PRIMUS IN ARMIS

PRIMUS IN ARMIS

ICH DIEN

PRINCE OF WALES OWN ROYAL REGIMENT

PRIMUS IN ARMIS

An Illustrated History of The Royal Wiltshire Yeomanry (Prince of Wales' Own Royal Regiment)

STEPHEN KEOGHANE

FONTHILL

Oh, it's sweet to sweat through stables, sweet to empty kitchen slops,
And it's sweet to hear the tales the troopers tell,
To dance with blowzy housemaids at the regimental hops
And thrash the cad who says you waltz too well.
Yes, it makes you cock-a-hoop to be 'Rider' to your troop,
When you envy, O how keenly, one poor Tommy being cleanly
Who blacks your boots and sometimes calls you 'Sir.'

'Gentlemen-Rankers'
Rudyard Kipling

Fonthill Media Language Policy

Fonthill Media publishes in the international English language market. One language edition is published worldwide. As there are minor differences in spelling and presentation, especially with regard to American English and British English, a policy is necessary to define which form of English to use. The Fonthill Policy is to use the form of English native to the author. Stephen Keoghane was born and educated in the United Kingdom; therefore, British English has been adopted in this publication.

Fonthill Media Limited
Fonthill Media LLC
www.fonthillmedia.com
office@fonthillmedia.com

First published in the United Kingdom and the United States of America 2020

British Library Cataloguing in Publication Data:
A catalogue record for this book is available from the British Library

ISBN 978-1-78155-789-1

Typeset in 10.5pt on 13pt Sabon
Printed and bound in England

A young RWY subaltern scanning the horizon in the Middle East in 1940.

The original five squadron colours, the regimental standard, and the drum banners. The squadron colours, the term used in Henry Graham's regimental history, were presented by Lady Bruce in 1798 to the 1st Squadron in Marlborough and Swindon, the 2nd from Devizes and Everleigh, the 3rd from Melksham and Warminster, the 4th from Malmesbury and Chippenham, and the 5th based in Hindon and Salisbury.

Foreword

I feel very honoured to have been asked to write the foreword to what is a quite remarkable book. It has been a labour of love for the author, a practising consultant surgeon, but also latterly the regimental medical officer for twenty-two years of the Royal Wessex Yeomanry. He has made his book a pilgrimage by carrying out painstaking research, tracking down descendants of old yeomen, interviewing them, and carefully going through many thousands of photographs. This brings many of the characters to life and of course makes it much more interesting to read, unlike many military histories and the rather dry annals of the official war diaries that describe with which formation the regiment was involved, when, and where etc. In this book, the characters often speak for themselves.

I have been particularly asked to try and explain why we do it, what the attraction of being a yeoman is, and why we serve, sometimes for many years. I think there are a variety of reasons that are perhaps not easy to define.

At the time of National Service, we were obliged to serve for three years on the reserve, and this compulsion soon became a pleasurable habit. Comradeship (which means, of course, abiding friendships) is made even more meaningful in times of danger, stress, or discomfort.

Why do we give up so much of our time to soldiering? In my own case, I worked in London indoors during the week, predominantly with women without at the time realising the antithesis was serving in the yeomanry being outdoors with men.

Personal pride comes into it—the urge to do better. Young officers and soldiers attending courses, often at the home of the Royal Armoured Corps in Bovington or Lulworth, would strive to achieve higher marks or do better than their Regular Army colleagues, which they frequently did.

When I was commanding, we were visited by no less a person than the chief of the general staff, who came to see us in the field and was rather sceptical of the abilities of the Territorial Army (TA). It was tipping it down with rain, I remember; he could not comprehend that we were using 'Griddle' and 'Slidex'—codes that we used every day in RHQ and SHQ.

He asked if he could visit an OP (observation post), so we climbed into my Land Rover and approached one from the rear; it was extremely well concealed. The general climbed on the back of the vehicle and asked the fat corporal if he was enjoying himself. Soaking wet, the corporal replied, 'well I wouldn't fucking well be here if I wasn't.' This unique breed is not afraid of top brass, yet he truly respects and supports his officers to the hilt; good discipline can and does operate within a friendly and informal environment.

I can recall being told a nice story that occurred in the desert when a visiting officer remarked to the colonel that the saluting in the regiment did not appear to be of a very high standard; to this, the colonel remarked, 'I've always found they tend to prefer a friendly wave'—an informal acknowledgement they probably picked up from their New Zealand comrades in arms.

The same names often crop up down the years—the Awdrys, Fullers, Herberts, and Thynnes. We have trained not only all over Salisbury Plain, but in the Cambrian Mountains, the North German Plain, Canada, and some of us in Iraq and Afghanistan. I have had the enjoyment and privilege of being a Wiltshire Yeoman serving for forty-two years and closely involved for a further twenty. It feels like a family regiment and has surely proved its value to county and country over 200 years.

Colonel David C. Part OBE TD DL
Former Commanding Officer of the Royal Yeomanry and Honorary Colonel of the Royal Wiltshire Yeomanry

Contents

Foreword 7
Introduction 11

1 The First Hundred Years of the Yeomanry Cavalry in Wiltshire 15
2 The Early 1900s and the South African War 27
3 The Great War 51
4 1918–1939 65
5 Mobilisation and the Middle Eastern Adventure 85
6 El Alamein: The Finest Hour 129
7 The Italian Campaign 152
8 Yeomanry Tales 159
9 The Post-war Era 185
10 'A' (RWY) Squadron, The Royal Yeomanry 201
11 'B' (RWY) Squadron, The Royal Wessex Yeomanry 220
12 Freedom Parades and the RWY Squadrons Reunite Under A New Cap Badge 238

Appendix: Tank Markings in the Middle East and Italy 244
Bibliography 255

Introduction

Two decades later, I can still recall with absolute clarity my recruitment into the Royal Wessex Yeomanry, which took place over a routine varicose vein operation in Stroud General Hospital, my predecessor being a local general practitioner anaesthetist. The days of young, trainee surgeons operating alone in small hospitals with the now-extinct species of the GP anaesthetist are long gone.

I spent the first half of my military career as a regimental medical officer serving with a Royal Gloucestershire Hussar squadron and ended my time at regimental duty with 'B' (RWY) Squadron the Royal Wessex Yeomanry (RWxY). However, I first came to visit the RWY some years before on a cold and wet evening in November 1991 when working in Salisbury; hence I started and ended my connection to the yeomanry in the county of Wiltshire. In 1944, the RWY ended their time in Bury St Edmunds in Suffolk, the town in which I now work; fate is indeed strange.

The power of the internet and social media have helped enormously in the preparation of this book, but as with every literary project, there are many people to whom I am eternally grateful.

Ben Adams and Jonathan Ford, with whom I had the pleasure to serve from the early 1990s, were the first to come forward with their own large photographic collections.

David Gadd, John Davis, Anthony Langdon, the late Reverend Adrian Heath, and Andrew Pulford's service with the RWY spanned sixty years, and they have generously donated images and anecdotes. Murph Carson, whose own military career covered four decades, and Fred Feltham, an ex-11th and Royal Hussar and PSI in Swindon, enthusiastically helped with the collection of material.

Colonel David Part's generosity and encyclopaedic knowledge of the RWY in the post-war period has added to the character of the book; sadly, I could not include some of his racier but highly entertaining anecdotes about selected officers. As part of my tour of Wiltshire collecting photographs, I also visited Colonel David Carson, the RWY archivist who provided the stunning images from the Devizes parade.

Perry Doner in Canada allowed me to trace David Jones, who very kindly provided photographs of his uncle (Lieutenant Nigel Carter), who died in Palestine in 1940.

Ron Murrell from the Moyes Museum in Bury St Edmunds provided an invaluable link to his cousin, Stephen Woodman, and the vast amount of unseen material relating to Sergeant Woodman MM. This in turn led to me meeting Peter and Christine Fuller, the family of Len Oakley, and Elizabeth Mann (daughter of Trooper Ted Bolton).

Malik Merchant and Taj Kothari from the Ismaili community in the USA provided information on the late Prince Aly Khan.

Rollo Clifford, who has published similarly on the Royal Gloucestershire Hussars, very kindly allowed me to access his own research on the Imperial Yeomanry in the South African War. Brigadier Robert Sutcliffe, the honorary colonel at the time of writing, enabled me to copy the Second World War collection of photographs of Lt Jimmy James, taken using a German camera and hence of a higher resolution than many period images.

The families of now-deceased yeomen from the two world wars have astounded me with their trust and generosity—Mark Williams, Sandra Allen, Ruth Jenkins, Terry Crawford, Stephen Hanney, James and Douglas Lawrence, Tamsin King, Richard Fisher, Judy Thomas, Ian Smith, Tim Daws, Chris Kemp, Keith Clifford, and Chris Strachan provided fascinating anecdotes that add to the individuals' stories.

Corporal Paul Cross, WO2 Neil Dackham, WO2 Darren Hill, Jim Martin, Lt-Col. Charles O'Neil Roe, Captain Wayne Price, Andy Turner, and Les Welsh (whom I served alongside for many years) were again sources of valuable information.

Major-General Simon Brooks-Ward, Lt-Cols Conn MacEvilly and Mike Dalzell, and Sergeant Mark Denman all provided first-hand accounts of the entry into Iraq in 2003.

Ian Chard is a leading expert on the yeomanry contribution to the long-range desert group (LRDG) and freely gave his time and the images he had accessed from original patrol members for publication.

Neil Ashley, Anthony Longdon, and Neil Stevens via his father David provided many of the atmospheric images and stories from the Cold War as did Alan Clarke from the Salisbury Museum.

The Wiltshire County Archive holds the regimental archive and Tom Plant efficiently co-ordinated the copying of a large volume of regimental material that was deposited some years ago by Colonel David Carson, himself a subject matter expert.

Dr Theo Bergenthal from the Villa Wessel Gallery in Germany generously advised on the paintings of Rommel's war artist, and Jerome Lantz in France allowed the use of many of the Victorian images from his comprehensive and detailed website Hussards-Photos.

Ian McHarg, who has published on No. 11 Commando in Syria, and Peter Green, who runs the *Oflag* IX website, were key to unravelling the story behind one of the regiment's Second World War officers.

The marquess of Lansdowne, Lord Methuen, Sir James Fuller, Andrew Christie-Miller, Rachel Thacker, Charles Bartholomew, and Colonel Charlie Blount all provided unseen information on their forefathers who had served in the regiment.

A day I will never forget and I feel eternally lucky to have experienced was the one I spent visiting Ken Batt and his wife, Joyce; Ken was the last RWY survivor from the battle of El Alamein.

Suzanne Foster and Tace Fox, the archivists at Winchester College and Harrow School, very kindly allowed the use of images from their collections, as did Gordon Shaw from the Rodbourne community group in Swindon.

Colonel Toby Bridge late KRH and Philippa Long generously proofread the final manuscript to perfection. If I have forgotten anyone, I sincerely apologise.

I have worked closely with one individual whom I believe deserves his own book; Tim Neate is a Wiltshire man and an accomplished photographer, model maker, graphic designer, and military author, who has spent decades studying the regiment's armoured vehicles. His knowledge of the RWY armour is unsurpassed and Tim has acted as a reliable and very welcome reference point throughout this project, enhancing many of the images in this book.

As every author should, I must thank my incredibly patient wife, Lizzy, who tolerated confiscation of the dining room table and my endless hours at the computer.

Stephen Keoghane
Suffolk 2019

1

The First Hundred Years of the Yeomanry Cavalry in Wiltshire

In 1794, there was a genuine fear in the country that an invasion by the French Revolutionary Army was imminent and that the existing standing or regular army was an insufficient deterrent. In response to this perceived threat, on 5 March, the prime minister, Pitt the Younger, for the first time used the phrase 'yeomen [*sic.*] cavalry' and the story of this regiment begins.

The Royal Wiltshire Yeomanry was commissioned on 12 May 1794 at the Bear Inn in Devizes, a town that continues to be its spiritual home; ten volunteer troops then came together under the command of Lord Bruce as a formation in 1797, these ten troops subsequently becoming five squadrons. Colours, later termed standards and guidons, were presented to the troops in June 1798 when a staggering twenty-eight officers and 564 men were on parade a mere two years after the call to arms. From the outset, the yeomanry was an exclusive organisation, an appointment as an officer being granted by the lord-lieutenant of the county.

In 1800, civil unrest began in Wiltshire initially as a response to a lack of grain and hence bread; this unrest would be a feature throughout the country as a whole for the next three decades and gave rise to the commanding officers of yeomanry regiments being at liberty to 'put down' riots. Silk weavers were the source of further unrest in 1816, necessitating the issuing of ammunition to the Salisbury and Hindon troops; by 1830, these civil disturbances had reached their peak.

The yeomanry was called out to face 500 rioters in West Tisbury over a number of days in November of that year; cavalry charges took place and order was restored, but many yeomen were injured and a rioter was shot dead by the troops. Peace was eventually restored in Wiltshire and as a result, the title 'Royal' was awarded in 1831—the first yeomanry regiment to be honoured in such a manner.

Thirty-three years later, the RWY provided an escort for the Prince of Wales, later HM King Edward VII, when he visited the marquess of Ailesbury in

Savernake Forest. This led to the title 'Prince of Wales' Own' and the adoption of the three feathers and the motto '*Ich dien*'.

In the late 1860s, the British Army, in a pattern that has continued throughout its existence, was in a rather sorry state, and the yeomanry as a whole faced disbandment in an attempt to save money. The volunteers survived this early defence review, but changes were needed. In 1870, new regulations abolished independent troops and a fixed regimental strength was specified as was a required number of training days throughout the year. The slack ways of the past would have to change, and even training for the adjutant and permanent staff was at last formalised as the regiment now became another element of the British Army as a whole.

Field training known as 'Field Days' and autumn manoeuvres continued, and in 1872, two 'armies' faced each other on exercise in southern England. The RWY was part of the Northern Army, with the order of battle consisting of 15,000 men, including seven regiments of cavalry, eighteen Royal Horse Artillery guns, twenty-four field guns, nineteen infantry battalions, and two companies of Royal Engineers.

The manoeuvres ended with both armies camped at Durrington, north of Salisbury, and many thousands of the public attended the parade at the end of the exercise to view the spectacle of tens of thousands of troops on parade in front of the Prince of Wales.

The dismounted yeomen carried in an 'Irish car' who first appeared in 1861, attached to the Devizes, Marlborough, Melksham, and Chippenham troops. (*Photograph courtesy of Salisbury Museum*)

A trooper wearing the uniform of 1858 holding a 'Monkey Tail' carbine as described by Henry Graham in his two-volume regimental history. In 1858, some further alterations were made to the uniform. The red stripes on the overalls were altered to white, as were the red facings on the tunic. The size of the shako was much reduced, and an upright 'shaving brush' red plume substituted for the white horse-hair one. The Westley-Richards 'Monkey Tail' carbine, an early breech-loading weapon, was introduced in 1870:

> Lord Ailesbury had a foot parade on the following Monday, and addressed the regiment. He said that Westley Richard carbines would shortly be issued, though for his part he did not see that they were wanted, as they had already a number of men armed with rifles.

That evening, at a formal dinner held at Tottenham House on the Savernake estate, the highly respected Regimental Sergeant-Major Pennistone fell from his chair in what was presumed to be a faint but was later pronounced dead by the regimental surgeon. Dinner continued to avoid upsetting the guests. The trooper illustrated above wears field day order as described in the rules and regulations of the RWY Cavalry, approved by the Right Hon. Garthorne Gathorne-Hardy, secretary of state for war in 1877.

The field day order stated:

> To be used generally for summer drills, divisional and brigade field days, garrison orderlies, mounted police in garrison and camp, and when specially ordered:
>
> Tunic, shako plumed and uncased, cap lines, gloves, pants, boots with spurs sword and sword belts, pouch and belt. Horses saddlery complete with cloak, sheepskin, wallets, collar chain and carbine. The cloak, when worn on the saddle, will be rolled forty inches in length.

The shako would eventually be replaced by a fur busby in 1880 as the regiment made the stylish transition to more fashionable hussars. (*Images from Hussards-Photos*)

The officers in stable dress at Warminster, 1861. *Standing:* Capt. H. Calley, Lt G. Sotheron-Estcourt, QM T. Iveson, Capt. Earl Nelson, unknown officer, Capt. A. L. Goddard, Capt. Lord C. Bruce, Lt W. C. Merriman, Capt. Lord Shelbourne, Lt Vere Fane Benett, Lt N. Barton, Lt W. Macdonald, RSM Pinnegan, and Lt H. Danby-Seymour. *Sitting:* Maj. Rt Hon. T. Sotheron-Estcourt, Capt. Sir F. H. Bathurst, Lt Lord H. Thynne, Capt. the Earl of Suffolk, Col. the Marquess of Ailesbury, Lt E. T. Clarkson, Capt. T. F. Grove, Maj. Lord E. Bruce, Lt D. Bennett, Lt E. Miles, Lt W. E. Matcham, and Lt G. P. Fuller.

This was the first year that the dismounted yeomen adopted by Lord Ailesbury accompanied the regiment for 'permanent duty' as annual camp was known. Two carts of twelve men were attached to each squadron, perhaps the precursor of an assault troop 100 years later.

However, in 1876, the government announced that yeomanry regiments were to take on the role of light cavalry, and these experimental riflemen recruited from the towns were to be scrapped.

Some notable officers of the late Victorian period included the following:

John Dickson-Poynder DSO, served with the Royal Scots (The Royal Regiment) prior to the RWY. He fought with the 1st Battalion of the Imperial Yeomanry in the Boer War and later became governor of New Zealand, undersecretary of state for India, and was titled Baron Islington.

Sir Thomas Fowler of Gastard near Corsham was born in 1868 and served with the Wiltshire Imperial Yeomanry in South Africa where he was shot in the thigh and subsequently died in April 1902 at the Battle of Moolman's Spruit. His memoirs were later privately published by his family.

Above: The date of this photograph is somewhere between 1865 and 1868 as shakos and a light dragoon pattern braided tunic are worn. Trumpet Major Rollands is pictured standing centre behind the earl of Suffolk. The original labelling of this faded photograph in the archive is incorrect but Lord Dangan (who was related to Arthur Wellesley), the duke of Wellington, and Lord Ailesbury are positively identified sitting to the right of Lord Suffolk. What these faded images reveal is that some of the most influential men in England were serving in the regiment at this time.

Below: Two troopers' *carte de visite* (CDV) by James Owen photographic studio in Salisbury. The uniform is dark blue with scarlet facings. Later tunics had six rows of braiding as per the regular hussar pattern. The CDV acted as the Facebook or Instagram of its day; the soldier was photographed in his smartest uniform and these postcard-sized images could be left as calling cards for family, friends, and sweethearts.

Above: Trooper 1890 by W. G. Honey, a photographer based in Devizes and Trowbridge, and a sergeant in 1882. (*Images from Hussards-Photos*)

Below: The officers wearing a variety of uniform in 1883. *Standing:* W. J. Grove, A. W. Neeld, Viscount Weymouth, Capt. H. Graham (Adjutant 16th The Queen's Lancers), B. Helme, Capt. Lord Bruce, Capt. W. H. Long, Sir H. B. Meux, and J. H. Sadler. *Seated:* G. P. Goldney, G. T. J. Sotheron-Estcourt, Sir E. H. Hulse, Col. Lord Bath, Capt. Lord Folkestone, C. N. P. Phipps, E. H. Clutterbuck, and Dr J. B. Maurice.

The Warminster troop, 1883. The officers to the right are C. N. P. Phipps and Lord Bath. Phipps was elected as the MP for Westbury in 1880. He married a Hervey-Bathurst and one of his daughters married Sir John Fuller of Neston Park; the Fuller family provided generations of regimental officers.

A mixture of braided patrol jackets and frock coats worn by the officers in 1887. *Standing:* Sir J. Kelk, T. R. Curtis, Capt. G. Watson-Taylor, Sir H. Pelly, C. N. P. Phipps, Lord Weymouth, Capt. W. H. Long, G. L. Palmer, and J. L. Fuller. *Seated:* Capt. B. Helme, Lt-Col G. T. J. Sotheron-Estcourt, Col. Lord Bath, and Capt. Sir A. W. Neeld. *Front row:* J. P. Goddard, Capt. Lord Frederick Bruce, Capt. H. L. Aylmer (adjutant 16th, the Queen's Lancers), and J. R. G. Gwatkin.

The Salisbury troop on parade in full dress in March 1892 outside the walls of the famous cathedral.

The officers in 1894 wearing a mixture of braided patrol jackets and the recently introduced, blue serge frock—a simple tunic cut like a Norfolk jacket. *Standing:* G. E. Mackay, J. Joicey, Lord Ludlow, Sir J. Dickson-Poynder, Sir A. W. Neeld, O. C. Maurice (surgeon), Lord Weymouth, G. L. Palmer, T. R. Curtis, Sir T. Fowler, and R. A. Poore. *Seated:* Sir H. B. Meux, W. H. Long, G. P. Goldney, Lord C. H. Bruce, Col. G. T. J. Sotheron-Estcourt, Capt. Scobell, J. P. Goddard, J. F. Stancomb, and J. R. G. Gwatkin.

Roger Poore was born in Bath in 1870, serving for twenty-four years in the RWY. He was awarded the DSO in South Africa and was mentioned in dispatches. He was killed in action during the Third Battle of Ypres in 1917 while commanding the 2nd Battalion, the Royal Welch Fusiliers, and is commemorated in St James' Church in Piccadilly as a member of Arthur's Club, one of the more exclusive but now dissolved London clubs.

In 1898, after eight years, Colonel Southeron-Estcourt relinquished command to Lt-Col. Long, whose first annual training period came under the scrutiny of no lesser a figure than Field Marshal Wolseley, commander in chief and the hero of most of the Victorian wars. To add to the ordeal, he was accompanied by a full general and a major-general.

The regiment, however, clearly made an impression as the commander in chief described them as 'ably commanded, with a satisfactory turn-out and the horses are of a good stamp, and the men know how to ride them'.

The year 1898 also saw vast army manoeuvres in the south of England involving over 50,000 troops; the Northern Army was under the command of HM Queen Victoria's son and career soldier, the duke of Connaught, while the Southern Army

Henry Ludlow Lopes, 1865–1922. A barrister and politician, he was gazetted a second lieutenant in the RWY in 1888 and, other than for a period of five years, served in the regiment until 1907. (© *Victoria and Albert Museum London*)

Above: Canal Street, Salisbury, 1892. This is a rare photograph demonstrating a white cover worn over the blue pillbox cap, possibly as protection from the elements or for fatigue duty to preserve the cloth and braid. The plain blue serge frock possibly issued in 1884 is worn. Annual training was based from Salisbury, but problems arose when it was discovered that a local cricket club had recently leased the proposed site of the regiment's camp and had laid a pitch. A generous donation from the regimental funds solved this dilemma.

Below: Officers of the Royal Gloucestershire Hussars (RGH) and the Royal Wiltshire Yeomanry. This unique image shows the RWY officers on the right of the photograph, wearing drill order with silver cross belts and silver bosses on their boots. In 1895, annual training was combined with the Royal Gloucestershire Hussars as both regiments were part of the 3rd Yeomanry Brigade.

The two regiments assembled at Cheltenham, drilling in Prestbury near the current national hunt racecourse with an impressive 270 all ranks on parade for the inspection by Colonel Gough, assistant inspector-general of Cavalry who pronounced himself 'highly pleased with the work and appearances of both regiments'.

Sgt Ashby from the RWY won the brigade prize for sword exercises beating a Gloucestershire Hussar, Sgt Vizard on home ground; the silver cup was presented by Maj. Wyndham-Quin, the brigade adjutant who served with the 16th the Queen's Lancers and the RGH. Wyndham-Quin later wrote a detailed regimental history of the RGH in 1898.

The following year, Devizes was the location for annual training. Colonel Sotheron-Estcourt commanded the 236 men who attended out of a total strength of 307. The year was marked by the death of the popular honorary colonel, the marquess of Bath who had joined the regiment in 1850 and was devoted to its wellbeing. The prominent politician the marquess of Lansdowne was then gazetted honorary colonel, having commanded the Chippenham troop from 1865–1873.

was led by the hero of the Zulu War Sir Redvers Buller VC. A second annual training fortnight put a huge strain on any regiment, but the RWY turned out an impressive thirteen officers and 220 men rather than the two squadrons that were initially anticipated.

For many reasons, these large-scale manoeuvres were not a great success; the armies were too close together at the start of the exercise, the daily cease fire was often at a key point in activities and significant transport and supply problems were encountered because these duties had been contracted to civilians. Despite these issues, the correspondent from *The Times* reported that 'the regiment had every reason to be proud of itself in this distinctly trying ordeal'.

Annual camp was spent in Weymouth with the Dorset (Queen's Own) Yeomanry although the two regiments saw little of each other, the RWY drilling at Chickerell and the Dorset on Lodmoor.

The RWY marched into the town on the day of Queen Victoria's eightieth birthday; the commanding officer's congratulatory telegram to Her Majesty included the line: 'from your premier yeomanry regiment'; her reply thanked, 'all ranks of the premier regiment of yeomanry for their kind message of loyal congratulations'.

Queen Victoria would later see a detachment of the regiment on parade when she visited Bristol in November of that year before the country's full attention was focused on South Africa.

Inspection by Field Marshal Viscount Wolseley in Devizes, June 1898.

The officers in 1899 in mounted drill order wearing blue serge tunics and scarlet and blue field service later termed 'side hats'. *Standing:* C. C. Gouldsmith, H. E. Spencer, J. Joicey, Sir T. Fowler, G. E. Mackay, O. C. Maurice, C. Bishop, Lord A. Thynne, G. Miles, E. Kingscote, D. Stancourt, R. A. Poore, J. R. G. Gwatkin, J. Bennet-Stanford, and Sir J. Dickson- Poynder. *Seated:* J. M. F. Fuller, J. P. Goddard, Sir A. Neeld, W. H. Long, Lord Bath, and G. Ll. Palmer. *Front row:* E. McNiven, E. S. Awdry, and C. M. Thornton. Of interest are the medical officers—Surgeon-Lieutenant Maurice wearing RWY uniform with a Royal Army Medical Corps cross belt and the Assistant Surgeon Kingscote wearing RWY uniform.

2

The Early 1900s and the South African War

In the early 1900s, change was still needed; Walter Long in his memoirs described some of the NCOs as 'splendid fellows but many were too old and stout to be able to work efficiently'.

The origin of this ruinously expensive and bloody war was independence from British colonial rule and the establishment of an independent republic. The British Army would face an enemy for whom they were simply not prepared, who was a patriot, a fine shot, and a good horseman. This era would force the red-and-blue-coated soldiers to learn a very different form of combat.

By December 1899, the War Office was faced with the difficult task of providing much-needed reinforcements of mounted troops. The marquess of Lansdowne, who was honorary colonel to the RWY, was the lead for proposing the utilisation of the yeomanry and rebranding them Imperial Yeomanry (IY). The reasoning behind the reinvention of this force was to circumvent the existing rules of engagement for yeomanry regiments that prevented them from serving overseas.

Two companies of men, who formed the 1st and 2nd Companies of the 1st Battalion of the Imperial Yeomanry, were raised in the county; a third would be formed later (63rd Company of the 16th Battalion). These new units were based at the artillery barracks in Trowbridge, where they underwent re-equipment and training, embarking for South Africa in March 1900.

On arrival in Cape Town in March 1900, the 1st IY moved to a concentration area at McKenzies Farm, 5 miles outside the Cape Colony where over 5,000 men from nine battalions were based. After some initial delays, on 16 April, the 1st and 2nd Companies moved inland from this rather unsatisfactory holding area, forming part of the 8th Division under the command of General Rundle, an artillery officer who had fought in most of Queen Victoria's wars. For much of the time, the companies acted independently, performing the traditional yeomanry duties of escorting and reconnaissance.

A detachment of the 2nd Company was in action in Senekal in the Orange Free State in May 1900 during which they captured a Boer flag that was presented to Colonel W. H. Long on their return home; a month later, all three companies took part in the campaign in the Orange Free State.

Further minor actions that involved casualties took place throughout the summer, and in September, a half company consisting of Captain Graves, Lieutenants Awdry and Henderson, and forty-one NCOs and yeomen were confronted by a force of some 3,000 Boers outside Ladybrand. The British garrison was besieged, having refused to surrender to the superior enemy force, and Corporal Blencoe from Devizes distinguished himself by using a broken mirror as an improvised signalling device that allowed a message to be received by the inbound relief force. The Boers intercepted this message and withdrew, having fired over 300 artillery shells into the isolated garrison.

Both companies were involved in a number of smaller actions, and in May 1901, the 1st IY was recalled to England under the terms of their engagement, having lost thirty-nine officers and men with many more invalided home sick or wounded.

The third of the RWY companies, the 63rd, departed for Africa in August 1901, deploying to Pretoria and for a time was besieged in the small town of Warmbads, thereafter taking part in several small and unsuccessful expeditions to clear the bushveld of enemy.

In January 1901, following a quiet spell in Pretoria, they were dispatched to Eastern Transvaal. A cat and mouse game around the Orange River followed, pursuing the Boer General De Wet, the finale being a cavalry charge on the Boer positions at Disselfontein; De Wet, however, escaped with 1,500 of his men.

Back at home, orders were received to continue with enlistment as the original companies were in such a sorry state due to illness and cross postings to locally raised units, including the South African Police. Quantity of recruits took precedence over quality, and there was great concern about the lack of training given to many of these new volunteers and the poor conditions in which they found themselves when they arrived for training in Aldershot. The newly commissioned junior officers were equally untrained, many of them having never worn a uniform. A letter home from Lieutenant Altham Graham-Clarke of the Gloucestershire Yeomanry explains this further:

> Here we are back again since I wrote my hurried scrawl to Frances just as we were going into Harrismith when as we thought, we were hurriedly turned around and ordered to overtake Brigadier Campbell and his Brigade of Guards.
>
> We made a forced march and overtook them and were going to Reitz. After we had gone some way we were turned off, ordered to push for Bethlehem where we arrived yesterday.
>
> We had an awful march for two days and nights with incessant rain and I have an awful cold in consequence. It appears they thought De Wet had reoccupied the place, I was sent on with six men in to the town to find out if the Boers were in and

> found it luckily clear. 200 were just outside and were coming in today, so we were just in time.
>
> Poor Stanley Clarke of the 2nd Wilts was killed near here last Sunday. He was sent out from here with half his squadron to round up some Boers and from what we can hear from native sources was shot through the stomach and died that night. He used to shoot at Fretherne and you may have met him. I only hope the name and Regt hasn't upset all of you. I can't wire as the telegraph machine here has been taken away and we are again cut off from the world.
>
> I have today been offered his squadron, the 2nd Wilts and don't know what to do. It will break my heart to go away from my own troop. I broke down today when discussing it with them, but at the same time I think I ought to take it. It means a show of my own and 5/- a day and of course captain's batta [*sic.*]. At present the Squadron is all over the country and in a very bad state.
>
> No officers, only Speke, all the others sick or invalided, but if I can do any good with them it will do me a lot of good with Walter Long and I might tumble into some soft job when this is over. They have had six men killed in the last ten days and this beastly round up job is I think a most dangerous one.
>
> They have let nearly all the Boers who surrendered go back to their farms and now they have dug up their other rifles and it strikes me very forcibly that this part will have to be thoroughly cleared out, man woman and child. We are getting very tired of it and bitter and a great many farms will be burnt down before many days are over. I think all these brutes have been treated much too leniently by what they call Intelligence Officers.

Writing from Harrismith in April, a soldier described in a letter home the journey of seven days spent in coal trucks in the rain before arriving at camp only to be criticised for their scruffy appearance.

The 63rd Company was recalled to England in May 1901, and the Wiltshire companies as a whole returned from the campaign in July that year. Soon, reports reached members of parliament and the local newspapers from disgruntled yeomen who had experienced arrears in their pay from the war; this has remained a source of irritation for returning volunteers ever since.

In August, a suntanned representative detachment of 120 officers and men wearing slouch hats and puttees paraded in St James' Street in London before marching to Horse Guards Parade, where during a two-hour ceremony, the Wiltshire yeomen were called forward as individuals to receive the new South African medal from HM the king.

The first of many banquets to celebrate their return was held in the Palace of Westminster and thereafter in hotels and the great houses of Wiltshire. The reception at Hartham Park, owned by Sir John Dickson-Poynder near Corsham, was attended by 224 returned soldiers and the *crème* of Wiltshire society with characteristically long and flowery speeches accompanied by applause and numerous toasts. The bond between men and officers was clearly significant as

the officers were goaded by their soldiers to make further speeches, the heartiness of the occasion being described as 'somewhat demonstrative' by Captain Speke. The medical officer reportedly thanked the men of the 1st Company for not troubling him unless they were 'absolutely obliged to do so'. On 8 August, Lord Frederick Bruce was recorded by the *Devizes and Wiltshire Gazette* as stating:

> the time would come when some serious questions would be asked of those who were responsible for a great deal that had happened in the last two years, and that they would have to stand their trial before the bar of the country.

Following the establishment of the commonwealth of Australia, the RWY as the senior yeomanry regiment was asked to provide two officers, two sergeants, and twenty-seven yeomen as part of the Imperial Representative Corps for an official visit to Australia.

Arriving in Freemantle a month after leaving the UK, there followed a series of parades and dinners that would continue throughout the country. More banquets, fine dining, tattoos, and fireworks followed a parade in Sydney on questionable horses, which entertained the locals by their behaviour; this routine was later continued in Brisbane. Festivities, however, came to a halt in Tasmania and then Melbourne as news reached the contingent of the death of HM Queen Victoria.

A rough voyage to the South Island of New Zealand and the second part of the tour included more parades and dinners and it is now difficult to imagine the excitement felt in the colonies when up to 10,000 people would turn out to watch the troops. The tired but well-fed contingent arrived back at Southampton in April 1901.

The officers prior to leaving England.

The Royal Horse Artillery Barracks in Trowbridge, 26 February 1900. The inspection of the Imperial Yeomanry with officers 'to the front'.

Above, below, previous and following page: Life under canvas at annual camp in the 1900s.

Regimental sword competition, 1900. 'Prize sword' was won by Tpr Wyatt from Salisbury.

Right: A studio portrait of four unnamed Imperial yeomen wearing a variety of uniform taken after the presentation in London as they are wearing the new Queen's South Africa medal.

Below: The Australian and New Zealand contingent in full dress, 1901.

A unique photograph showing the RWY mounted in full dress on parade in Sydney, commanded by Maj. Goddard and Lt Fuller. The enormous civil and military parade marked the start of the new century and the birth of Australia as a nation.

'C' Squadron under the command of Maj. Fuller in Perham Down, 1901.

COLONEL G. T. J. SOTHERON-ESTCOURT
(LORD ESTCOURT).
1890-1898.

Colonel G. T. J. Sotheron-Estcourt 1839–1915. Following the marquess of Bath's resignation due to a combination of ill health and other duties, George Sotheron-Estcourt was promoted to commanding officer in 1890. He served until 1898 handing over to Lt-Col. W. H. Long. He served as the MP for Wiltshire North 1874–1885 and died in 1915 when his barony then became extinct.

Back in England, the commanding officer clearly had mixed views on the performance of his regiment following this camp in 1901, as his rather long-winded five-page letter to his officers reveals. Many of the points raised could apply equally to the management of soldiers and the movement of Land Rovers or armoured vehicles 100 years later:

1. The officer commanding desires to call the attention of the officers of the Regiment to the following comments upon the work done in the field and in camp during the recent training at Perham Down, in the hope that they may lead to still greater improvement in the future.

2. A decided change for the better was observable in all respects this year as compared with last but there remains still, naturally, considerable room for improvement, due as regards the field work, to the fact that it is not only new but involves in many respects the complete reversal of what regiments have been taught the past years; and in regard to camp duties to the fact that senior officers never themselves enjoyed the advantages which are now at the disposal of subaltern officers, by having themselves to carry out as subordinates the various duties of camp life.

3. The field work was on the whole admirably carried out. The most noticeable fault was the tendency on the part of officers commanding squadrons not to push on with sufficient rapidity when the ground was open and the scouting consequently easy, and when there was comparatively speaking no difficulty maintaining touch between contiguous squadrons; when cover or broken ground containing deep valleys have to be passed, the pace must be regulated accordingly, or risk is run of the

scouting being inefficiently performed, and the presence of the enemy not detected, but when the country is open, the pace should be at once increased, and sometimes even to a steady gallop, the officer commanding the squadron taking care that the connection between his men and the adjacent squadron or squadrons is never lost.

4. The object in view and the formation adopted to obtain it should always be clearly explained to all the officers, permanent staff and section leaders before starting.

5. On no account should an officer, NCO or man be allowed to start on any detached duty or with a message unless he thoroughly understands what are his particular duties and what is required of him.

6. The officer commanding noticed more than once when attacks were made on positions, that the men were allowed to climb to the top of the hill remaining erect until they reached the ridge, the consequences being that for some minutes they could be seen along the top, and of course offer an easy target to the rifles of a concealed enemy. They should be instructed to lie down just before they reach the top of the ridge and crawl to the top and look over. In this way they conceal themselves from the enemy and are at the same time able to view the position in front of them.

7. As a rule, the led horses were very well managed. The officer or NCO in charge of the led horses should always remember it his duty to keep them out of the range of fire, and within easy reach of the dismounted men, and to keep them moving, so that in the event of their becoming momentarily exposed to the fire of the enemy, there will be less chance of casualties.

8. If the officer or NCO in charge of the led horses finds himself exposed to the enemy's fire he should at once increase the interval and distance between the sections, so causing a smaller target to be presented to the enemy, and move rapidly under cover if possible or out of effective range.

9. The men should be warned to go around roots clover and seed and generally to avoid doing any damage; they should be cautioned that they must be civil to any civilian who may object to their presence, or with whom they may come in contact in the course of their operations.

10. It is of the utmost importance that officer commanding squadrons should arrange for as much rifle practice as may be possible before the training commences. It is also desirable that during the winter months arrangements should be made for the Permanent Staff to give instruction in riding and the putting on of saddles, bridles etc. It is only necessary to have ten or fifteen men present and four or five horses. If each man has a quarter of an hour or twenty minutes instruction as often as may be possible, he would very soon learn how to care for and saddle his own horses, and obtain a correct seat.

11. Men should be constantly practiced in mounting and dismounting with rifles. Rapidity in these movements is of the greatest importance.

12. With regard to camp duties, the chief mistake made was the failure on the part of the troop officers to look after their men and horses. If possible, an officer should be made responsible for each troop in the squadron—if there are not sufficient officers it may be necessary to put two troops under one officer detailing a sergeant to assist him in each case. The troop officer must be responsible for the general efficiency of his troop, for the care of the men and of the horses, and it should be his

business to see that as many men as possible of his troop are on parade every day. The most important time or the performance of these duties is immediately on the return of the Regiment from the field.

If the men are wet it should be his business to see that arrangements are made for drying their clothes, and that they do not remain in wet clothes. He should also take care that saddles are not removed until the backs are dry and cool so that the lining and padding of saddles are properly cared for, that horses' shoes are right, heels dried etc. and that the horses are fed with an intelligent regard for their individual requirements. It is also his business to see the tents are properly cleaned and tidied, everything neatly folded and put in its correct place.

13. Troop officers should select the most capable man of each section to act as section commander. They should hold the section commander responsible both in camp and in the field for the work of his section.

14. It is important that officers should make the NCOs realise that promotion brings with it responsibilities, and they will not be allowed to retain their stripes unless they do their work efficiently. An NCO should not be content to give orders to his men, it should be his business to set an example in punctuality, smartness and general efficiency and no trooper should be recommended for promotion unless his officers are satisfied that he has deserved it and can be relied upon to do his duty.

15. The improvement which has been manifested in the Regiment in the short time that has elapsed since they first went into camp shows how easy it is to attain a much greater degree of perfection if only sufficient attention is paid to the work, and enough trouble taken.

The officer commanding is confident he can rely upon his officers to assist him in bringing the Regiment to a very high standard of efficiency and smartness.

October 1901

The sergeants wearing blue patrol jackets with chain mail at annual camp in the early 1900s.

In 1902, the first attempts at modernising the yeomanry and imposing new terms and conditions of service materialised although this had little practical effect on the regiment and the annual training cycle continued much as it had done before the South African War. In March 1902, the newly titled prince and princess of Wales were met at Chippenham station and escorted with the duke of Beaufort to the county boundary where the RWY was relieved of escort duties by the Royal Gloucestershire Hussars. Interestingly, the regimental archive refers to the visit of the duke and duchess of York since in 1902, Prince George (later to become King George V) unusually held both titles.

The regimental band. The ornate kettle drums on the grey still exist on display in the Army Reserve Centre in Swindon.

RSM A. Lawrence (later quartermaster to the RWY) is shown bottom right standing next to the mounted escort, which was commanded by Lt R. F. Fuller. In the foreground, a company of the 2nd Volunteer Battalion the Wiltshire Regiment present arms.

Officers of the Royal Wiltshire Imperial Yeomanry, 1903. *Standing:* Capt. The Earl Cardigan DSO, Capt. G. Mackay, 2Lt Mann, 2Lt B. Lamb, Lt Lord Ludlow, 2Lt R. Fuller, Lt F. H. Fair, 2Lt R. Awdry, 2Lt W. Yeatman-Biggs, Lt C. S. Awdry, Lt C. M. Thornton, 2Lt E. A. Beavan, Lt S. C. Grant, and Lt E. R. Cox. *Sitting:* QM T. H. Deacon, Capt. J. Joicey, Lt N. Fuller, Capt. W. F. Collins (Adjutant the Royal Scots Greys), Maj. F. R. P. Goddard, Col. Rt Hon. W. H. Long, Maj. the Marquess of Bath, Maj. J. M. F. Fuller, Dr Leith (acting medical officer), and Maj. Sir J. Dickson-Poynder MP.

Lt-Col.Walter Long was an experienced politician, having been elected as a member of parliament for North Wiltshire 1880–85, for the Devizes Division from 1885–92, for West Derby from 1892–1900, and finally for South Bristol in 1900. His great grandfather was high sheriff when the regiment was formed, and Long received his commission from Lord Ailesbury, son of the man who raised the RWY.

In his memoirs published in 1923, he described his early years when there were issues with discipline with little effort being made by officers to learn their work. 'Exercises for Field Days' were written on cards, and if the CO changed his mind on the day, the officers under him as likely as not failed to realise what was happening with resulting chaos. Life in the yeomanry was certainly leisurely, and all sorts of uniform appeared on morning parades, which never took place before 10 a.m.

Walter Long joined his Warminster troop in 1876 when it was commanded by Mr Barton, a small, country squire. When Long asked him what to do when riding in column, the troop leader, not knowing any better, suggested riding at the head of the column to avoid the dust.

Long recalled later being told by an old, rather magnificent-looking trumpeter (who, although looking the part, could not sound a note) not to listen to the sergeant-major but to stand still behind the flagpost during a march past, again to avoid dust.

In 1877, the War Office discovered that the RWY was poorly recruited, and unless it could be strengthened, it faced disbandment. Lord Bath then wrote to Walter Long to ask if he could raise a contingent from his tenants and neighbours to bolster the struggling Warminster troop. Without the help of a regular officer or senior NCO, sixty-four yeomen were recruited, and in November 1877, they formed the Rood Ashton troop.

Sergeant-Major Bosworth of the 5th (Princess Charlotte of Wales) Dragoon Guards became the first instructor, remaining with the RWY until he retired to run a club in Moryhampton. Long describes him as 'not what is ordinarily known as a smart soldier', but he was devoted to his task and his soldiers; he was also a highly knowledgeable cavalryman.

The Rood Ashton troop subsequently grew to squadron size and for many years won the regimental prizes for swordsmanship and shooting, even competing at the naval and military tournament in London; by 1923, there was a waiting list to join the troop.

The uniform was described as 'varied' and NCOs were elected by the troop and chosen generally not because of their knowledge or efficiency but because they were popular characters or occupied leading positions at home among the troopers.

On a particular field day in the presence of the duke of Cambridge, the regiment was ordered to charge; with the men being untrained as were, the horses almost ran down the duke.

Long volunteered the regiment to deploy as a formed unit to South Africa, but the offer was declined and the War Office decreed that instead he should raise a squadron of mounted infantry. He contacted Lord Landsdowne and asked to utilise the empty royal artillery barracks at Trowbridge, which was occupied within two hours of permission being granted. Workmen appeared to restore the tired buildings, but the CO, unhappy with the pace, offered to bring in his own workmen from the family estate, resulting in the barracks being ready sooner than expected.

In under ten days, there were 1,700 applicants for a squadron, the total strength of which was to be 120. Many of the applicants had no idea how to hold a carbine but almost without exception claimed to be capable and experienced horsemen, although a few who exaggerated their equestrian experience mounted from the wrong side and were found to be wholly ignorant of the horse.

His adjutant, a key individual, soon reported sick and Sergeant-Major Lawrence (later captain and quartermaster) took over the important duties, succeeded by Captain Stack, unusually an Indian Army cavalry officer.

The squadron bought its own tack from the leather centre of Walsall using a grant from the War Office supplemented by a £7,000 fund that was fundraised from the county that was to be split between the RWY and infantry.

Soon, the squadron outgrew the new barracks and relocated to an old mill above the banks of the River Biss, and Lord Bath took over as second in command and took on a lot of work as CO, as Long's duties as an MP and cabinet member increased.

Capt. H. J. Tilney, the attached adjutant from the 14th King's Hussars and Quartermaster Deacon at Burderop Park camp near Swindon in May 1904. Tilney's grandson, who served with the 14th/20th King's Hussars and the King's Royal Hussars, commanded the RWxY in the late 1990s.

Sgt George Deacon mounted on Barnam and winner of the regimental jumping competition on 29 May 1907. Deacon and Son is a well-known and historic Swindon jeweller and clockmaker founded in 1848. Sgt Deacon served in South Africa but died of tuberculosis in 1913. (*Image courtesy of Deacons jewellers*)

A period cartoon describing rather damp and unfavourable training conditions familiar to all Wiltshire yeomen.

An officer's inspection, *c.* 1900. Note the variety and lack of uniformity of headdress on display.

Annual Camp, Uffington in Oxfordshire, May 1905. *Rear rank:* A. Henderson, C. S. Awdry, W. H. Mann, W. F. Fuller, and B. Lamb. *Standing:* Rev. W. L. Waugh, R. Fuller, Dr Leith, Lord Alex Thynne, C. M. Thornton, Lord Ludlow, E. Richardson Cox, R. W. Awdry, and S. C. Grant. *Seated:* G. E. Mackay, T. H. Deacon, M. J. Fuller, H. J. P. Tilney (adjutant), Lord Bath, W. H. Long, G. Ll. Palmer, Sir J. Dickson-Poynder, and O. U. Thynne.

The officers are wearing an unusual and short-lived khaki tunic buttoned to the neck, which was a pre-cursor to service dress as worn at the front nine years later. If it had remained in service, it may have proved a more practical uniform than wearing a collar and tie in the field. It was in this year that the king authorised the first long-service medal for ten years of continuous duty.

The officers in Warminster, 1907, wearing blue tunics cut in the style of later khaki service dress with hunting stocks in place of a collar and tie.

The white cap bands denote enemy forces on manoeuvres somewhere in England and the shoulder title is the post-1908 letter 'T' over 'Y' over Royal Wilts of the newly created Territorial Force.

Shepherds Shore near Devizes in May 1908. *Standing:* P. Methuen, R. F. Fuller, B. H. A. Hankey, E. E. Seldon, Capt. Lord A. G. Thynne, T. H. Deacon, Col. H. M. Graham, W. F. Fuller, E. R. Cox, Dr O. Maurice, G. F. Buxton, C. S. Awdry, and Dr Leith. *Seated:* Maj. U. O. Thynne, Lt-Col. Palmer, Col. Lord Bath, Capt. B. Ritchie (Adjutant 15th King's Hussars), Maj. J. M. Fuller, and Capt. C. M. Thornton. *Front row:* R. W. Awdry, M. H. Beaujoy, B. Lamb, A. L. Palmer, and W. H. Mann. Note the two medical officers, one wearing RWY uniform and the other a locally employed physician.

The regimental band wearing full dress tunics with blue-and-red-peaked forage caps.

The aftermath of the war in South Africa and the increasing concern about a potential war in Europe led to the first of the twentieth century's defence reviews. The yeomanry regiments had enjoyed autonomy and significant independence throughout their existence, and together with the regular army, they would be reorganised under plans drawn up by Richard Burdon Haldane, the minister for war.

Reformation was not an easy task as many of the regiments, particularly the RWY, were well-connected and included numerous MPs among the serving and retired officers. A new County Association was formed to deal with the administration and recruitment of volunteers but also to attract ex-regular servicemen into the Territorial Force.

Under the new reforms, the RWY dropped the descriptive term 'Imperial' and became part of the newly formed 1st South-Western Mounted Brigade together with the North Somerset Yeomanry, the Hampshire Yeomanry (Carabaniers), and the Hampshire Battery Royal Horse Artillery.

Troops were formally amalgamated to form squadrons, and although the pattern of annual training continued as before, combined training with infantry and artillery became a novel and not always welcome concept to many of the yeomen.

Regimental headquarters was now at Chippenham with squadrons and outlying troops spread throughout the county. The pattern of training throughout the year remained unchanged with a two-week annual camp still being the focus; for many, this acted as the annual holiday and a chance to spend time away from wives and children.

An important statement by General (later Field Marshal) Douglas Haig, who assisted Haldane in the reforms was that the Territorial Force was itself not an army, but in the event of war and with adequate training, it could become one.

In 1909, the first of the large-scale exercises involving the newly formed South Western Mounted Brigade and regular cavalry regiments took place in Wiltshire, which was based upon a real conflict in the Russo–Japanese War. A year later, the yeomen were deploying on manoeuvres carrying full marching order under the gaze of many of the generals who would command on the Western Front five years later. In 1911, the marquess of Bath, who had completed the required five years as CO, was succeeded by Lt-Col. Llewellyn Palmer.

The training years passed as they had for decades, but in 1914, with war looming, during annual camp near Tisbury, the emphasis during field training changed to basic soldiering skills and dismounted work in preparation of what was expected to follow, described by the Wiltshire Times as 'the biggest battle in the history of the world'. As the soldiers returned to their families in May, there was a certainty among them that they would soon be together again.

Warminster in 1911. Note the variation in uniform, with khaki service dress slowly replacing a variety of blue patrols.

The regimental funeral of Cpl Brown from the Warminster troop in 1909.

The Salisbury troop looking exceptionally smart in blue tunics with leather bandoliers.

Warminster in May 1911. *Standing:* B. Lamb, R. E. O. Long, J. A. Garton, Maj. C. S. Awdry, A. Henderson, and W. H. Mann. *Seated:* A. Ll. Palmer, Maj. R. A. Poore, Maj. U. O. Thynne, Lt-Col. G. Ll. Palmer, Maj. A. Thynne, and Maj. W.J. Fuller. This rare image shows an officer group wearing the short-lived but very elegant braided 'Egyptian style' tunic, similar to that worn by British officers serving in the Bengal Cavalry and produced as a substitute for full dress.

3

The Great War

Orders for mobilisation were received on 4 August 1914, and the following day, the squadrons assembled at Chippenham, Warminster, Devizes, and Swindon, wearing a variety of khaki and blue uniforms and even civilian suits.

A move took place by train to Winchester, wherein the college, a plaque still records the soldiers and their horses who were billeted overnight in those ancient buildings. From Hampshire, there was a further move to Sussex for many months of training under the command of the new CO, Lt-Col. Ulric Thynne, where the loss of 'C' Squadron and the redistribution of the men between the remaining three squadrons resulted in the regiment now having the same organisation as a regular cavalry unit.

Training in earnest really only began in the autumn of 1915, and Regimental HQ and 'D' (Swindon) Squadron finally reached France in December that year, earning them the 1915 Star. The remaining squadrons arrived in France in 1916; they were dispersed and attached to different organisations until November, when at last they were reunited as a formed regiment as part of XV Corps.

The original intention of using cavalry on the Western Front was to exploit the gains made by the infantry, but it was now clear that France was not a place for the mounted arm, and the squadrons were utilised for many less glamourous roles, including digging trenches.

A confident-looking troop in 1914.

The officers with visiting staff in the hutted camp in Forest Row, Sussex, in December 1914. Lt-Col. Ulric Thynne is seated in the centre of the photograph.

Scenes from the cloisters of Winchester College. (*Photographs attributed to the Headmaster and photographer M. J. Rendall, the Warden and Scholars of Winchester College*)

Sgt Harry Moors far right in the sergeants' mess.

Pte Fredrick Hinton, seen in 1915, who died in 1981. Frederick and his brother, Edgar, shown below enlisted following a recruiting event organised by their father in Upper Wanborough near Swindon and the two brothers remained with the regiment until they transferred to the 6th Battalion Wiltshire Regiment. Fred was captured in March 1918 and imprisoned in Schweidnitz Camp in Silesia but was unaware that Edgar had been killed during the German offensive of Operation Michael and rather poignantly Fred continued to ask about him in letters home to his mother.

The Moors family have an extraordinary connection to the regiment. George Moors was born in Dorset but worked as a farrier in Trowbridge, enlisting in the regiment in October 1914 at the advanced age of fifty-nine when he was rapidly promoted to farrier quartermaster sergeant. He transferred to the newly formed Labour Corps in 1917. Two of his sons, Henry and Edward, also served in the regiment.

Henry, pictured in full dress, joined the RWY in 1908 at Trowbridge and served throughout the First World War despite medical problems resulting in numerous hospital admissions. He was obviously a keen soldier, as when discharged in 1919, he re-enlisted in the Royal Army Veterinary Corps where he worked as an instructor in the farrier's school in Aldershot. Edward was in training until 1916 but transferred to the 11th Hussars (PAO) and left the army in 1919 to work with horses at a local brewery.

Cpl Edward Moors displaying his farrier's badge above his chevrons and the Imperial Yeomanry badge on the right breast. Edward Moors met his future wife when under training in England. Ellen worked at a nearby country house and accompanied her friend who had a date arranged with Edward's brother, Henry. Although initially not a great success (she recorded being 'bored stiff' with Edward's conversation), they married in 1919, but her new husband died in his sleep six weeks after the birth of their daughter six years later.

Edward Moors first on the left on fatigue duty with the regimental chefs.

Right: An extraordinary photograph of Edward and Henry's sister Margaret in Trowbridge wearing her brother's uniform. 'What do you think of me now I am a soldier' was the inscription on the back of the photograph.

Below: A squadron led by Maj. W. F. Fuller as part of 40th Division is inspected by HM King George V at Farnham in 1916.

William Robert Cowdrey was born in Devizes in 1894 and joined the RWY underage, later transferring to the mounted military police. After the war, he trained as a butcher and had a shop in Devizes before moving to the village of Littleton Panell in 1939. He died in 1975.

Sir Geoffrey Kelsall Peto with his troop in 1915. Peto was born in 1878; like many officers throughout the yeomanry, he was educated at Eton College and gazetted a second lieutenant in November 1915, eventually reaching the rank of captain. Appointed CBE in 1919, he was Member of Parliament for Frome between 1924 and 1929.

He spoke in the House of Commons on numerous issues, including communist propaganda and workers' rights, but also on more obscure topics, such as the benefit of oranges from the colonies over those imported from Palestine.

Left to right: Capt. M. L. Lakin, 11th Hussars (PAO) (adjutant); Capt. Edwards, 9th Lancers (former adjutant); Lt-Col. U. O. Thynne; Maj. Lord Alexander Thynne; and Lt E. P. Awdry (assistant adjutant) outside the orderly room in 1915. Lord Alexander Thynne was awarded the DSO but killed in action two months before the armistice in 1918.

From the regimental aid post where the yeomanry medical officer would administer first aid, the casualty would be transferred to a dressing station for triage and further treatment. The principles of casualty evacuation from the point of wounding at the time of this extremely rare photograph of an RWY ambulance changed very little until the conflict in Iraq in the early twenty-first century.

These pages: The youth of Wiltshire in the First World War.

Above: Oscar Spanswick from Burbage mounted on a doctor's large hunter. Oscar joined the regiment in 1910 aged fifteen years and eleven months, but like many, his attestation papers incorrectly list him as eighteen. He was released from military service in 1916 and spent his entire life in rural Wiltshire, rather aptly running 'The Prince of Wales' public house, where this photograph hung until 1948.

Opposite left: Herbert (Jack) Harrison was born in Salisbury in 1895. He worked for the family butcher's firm and enlisted in the Salisbury troop of 'A' Squadron in 1913. He served in England until June 1916 and was one of the many Wiltshire Yeomen who eventually found themselves as line infantry in the 6th Wilts. He was declared missing, presumed killed on the third day of the German spring offensive of 1918; like so many, he has no known grave, but his sacrifice is commemorated on the Arras memorial. His two brothers, one of whom served in the same regiment, thankfully survived the horrors of the First World War and lived to enjoy old age.

Opposite right: Donald Maurice Freeth (528374) was working as an apprentice at the GWR works in Swindon prior to enlistment in 'D' Squadron. A talented horseman and the CO's bugler, he was fortunate to be allocated a polo pony as his mount. Donald was lucky to survive the war; he witnessed his brother, Hubert, also serving in the regiment, survive a bayonet wound; lost part of a finger at Ypres; and survived a mustard gas attack.

In April 1918, while serving at Company HQ with the 6th Wilts, he recalled the death of Lord Alex Thynne, his CO who had taken shelter in a shell hole that then received a direct hit. He married his sweetheart Alice in 1922 and remained in the RWY, ending his army career as a major. Every year, he played the 'Last Post' at the Swindon Cenotaph on Remembrance Day.

The winter of 1916–17 was harsh, with six weeks of continuous frost taking its toll on the horses, but in March, despite bitterly cold conditions, the regiment played its only part as a mounted unit following the Germans on their retreat towards the small town of Clery (midway between Amiens and St Quentin), where they now encountered death, decay, and mud in pouring rain.

Patrols engaged German lancers (Uhlans), but by the end of March 1917, the horses were suffering, and as a formed unit, the RWY took no part in further action, withdrawing to defend the Flanders coast where the officers even managed to play polo on the beach.

On 3 September 1917, the RWY's time as a mounted regiment came to an end as they were posted to No. 3 Infantry Base Depot at Rouen, and later, fourteen officers and 232 men were absorbed into the 19th Division, gaining a new title—the 6th (Wiltshire Yeomanry) Battalion Wiltshire Regiment. Now acting as infantry, they served at Ypres in late 1917, then Bapaume and Messines Ridge in the early spring of 1918.

At Bapaume, the 6th was in action for a week, retreating before a numerically superior German force. Among the 500 casualties were Lt-Col. Lord Thynne (Ulric), who was wounded, and his successor, Major Awdry, who was killed two days later. In May that year, due to the overwhelming casualties, it was decided to disband the Battalion.

Two second-line units were also raised during the First World War. The 2/1st RWY was formed in 1914 as a training unit and formed part of the 2nd/1st South Western Mounted Brigade. Like many other second-line regiments, they moved frequently from camp to camp in the UK, eventually serving as cyclists, but by November 1916, they were broken up and joined the North Somerset Yeomanry as the 10th (Wiltshire and North Somerset) Yeomanry Cyclist Regiment based in Ipswich. This new nomenclature did not last long, and the RWY identity was restored in March 1917 with the regiment seeing out the remainder of the war in Dublin.

The third-line regiment, which was formed in 1915 as the 3/1st RWY, was never at full strength and its function was as a holding and training unit, the destination for the men eventually being the infantry as part of the Wiltshire Regiment.

Major C. S. Awdry, D.S.O.

South African medal) Wilts Yeomanry attached 6th Wilts Regiment), 19th Divi-
sion, Third Army, who was one of the two yeomanry officers present at the Siege of Lady-
brand in September, 1900, has been wounded and missing since March 25. He is believed to have passed through Rastatt, Russen Lager. Any information regarding him will be wel-
comed by Messrs. W. H. Smith and Sons,

Above left: Maj. Allan Llewelyn Palmer MFH (1883–1916). Originally commissioned into the 14th King's Hussars, he served with distinction in South Africa and later in India; he was joint master of the Cattistock Hounds in Dorset.

He joined the RWY in 1908, and at the outbreak of war, he was serving as a staff captain in Brigade Headquarters but was later appointed to command 'D' Squadron. An expert horseman and a keen hunting man as expected of any yeomanry officer, he could be seen jumping any available fence as the troops practised their mounted drills. He died in hospital in Amiens following a bout of appendicitis. He was the longest-serving squadron leader in the First World War and was greatly missed by his men. (*Photograph Harrow School collection*)

Above right: Maj. Charles Selwyn Awdry was born in 1877. He was educated at Winchester and New College, Oxford, joining the regiment in 1898. On the outbreak of the South African War, he deployed to the Cape with No. 1 Company of the 1st Imperial Yeomanry and was subsequently mentioned in despatches. In 1904, he became a partner in the firm W.H. Smith. Awarded a DSO when commanding the 6th Battalion the Wiltshire Regiment in the First World War, he was reported missing at Bapaume on the Western Front on 25 March 1918.

4

1918–1939

Following its disbandment at the end of the First World War, the regiment was re-established in 1920 with squadrons in Warminster, Devizes, and Chippenham. Remarkably, only twelve months later, the RWY was back at full strength—an incredible effort considering the weariness for warfare in the country.

Annual camp was reinstated taking place in Weymouth in 1922, and the following year, HRH the Prince of Wales inspected his regiment at Wilton House, the seat of the earl of Pembroke. Among the great families of Wiltshire, the Herberts, Fullers, Thynnes, and Awdrys continued to provide senior officers to the RWY throughout the 1920s and '30s.

In 1926, there was unrest in the country, not quite on the scale witnessed 100 years prior, but it led to the extraordinary measure of the RWY transferring to the regular army for a period of ninety days, tasked with carrying out essential tasks in Wiltshire at a time when many public services were threatened by general strike action.

The drill hall at Trowbridge was finally completed in 1927, with the town acting as headquarters for the regiment for decades to follow. Annual training continued unmodified, although in the early 1930s, at a time of great economic recession, there were significant financial restrictions placed on training; eighty years later, nothing had changed.

A key figure was the new adjutant, Captain St. George, who was posted from the Life Guards and would remain with the regiment throughout mobilisation and into Palestine. Many of the regimental officers were based outside the county and rarely seen—a phenomenon that would continue with the modern yeomanry regiments during the author's service.

The political situation in Europe and military technology were rapidly changing, but in rural England, the yeomanry continued with a pattern of mounted training that had remained essentially unchanged for a hundred years. In 1936, the king died, and the royal honorary colonel temporarily became monarch.

The entire regiment carried out mounted drills on Weymouth beach in May 1922.

The sergeants' mess at Wilton Camp, 1923.

Marlborough Camp, 1928. This was a private visit by the Prince of Wales, later King Edward VIII. His Royal Highness spent the night under canvas, having that day ridden back to camp at the head of his regiment. Gen. Sir Alexander Godley GOC Southern Command accompanies the commanding officer, Lt-Col. Mann.

The sergeants and warrant officers at Forest Hill Camp, Marlborough, May 1928. *Rear rank:* Farrier Sgt G. Smith, Sgt G. R. Payne, Sgt E. A. Bull, Sgt W. G. Hawkins, Sgt A. W. Fox, Sgt S. W. Oliver, Sgt W. H. Haynes, Sgt W. B. Freeth, Farrier Sgt R. F. Petty, Farrier Sgt A. G. Gurd, and Sadler Sgt L. G. Stagg. *Middle row:* Sgt C. Brown, Sgt H. R. Stiles, Sgt A. Haynes, SSM B. Pearson, SQMS H. J. Phillips, SQMS R. J. N. Sutcliffe, SQMS A. T. P. Luxtom MM, SQMS G. Grant, SSM H. Norman, Sgt H. G. Freeth, Sgt J. J. S. Webster, Sgt S. C. Butt, and Sgt W. Whitehorn. *Seated:* Sgt Trumpeter D. M. Freeth, QMS J. Williams, SSM C. D. Mead, SSM E. H. Northover, RSM S. B. Haines DCM, Lt-Col. W. H. Mann MC TD, HRH The Prince of Wales (Col. in chief), Capt. A. B. P. L. Vincent MC 3rd/6th DG (adjutant), RQMS G. Ellison, FQMS S. Mills, SSM W. F. Pickford, Bandmaster G. H. Freeth, and SSM W. A. Tilley.

The newspaper cutting read: 'The Salisbury troop, part of A Squadron grooming their mounts after operations at a camp near Winchester.' The year was 1933 when annual camp was held at Sparsholt and the CO hosted a tour of his old school Winchester College, where the regiment had been billeted in the First World War. With political change in Germany, recruits were now compelled by a new law to accept overseas service.

Lt-Col. E. P. Awdry (centre) took command in 1932. Maj. the Hon. Eric Long, regimental second in command who served for twenty-four years, is on his left (later Viscount Long of Wraxhall).

Sparsholt Camp, May 1933. *Left to right*: Maj. A. A. Bankier, 'C' Squadron leader who had served in the Royal Field Artillery in the First World War and was gazetted a lieutenant in the RWY in 1920, leaving in 1937; Lt C. E. Awdry; and Maj. the Hon. R. E. O. Long, regimental second in command.

The monotonous task of cleaning tack.

Mounted tug of war—an unusual equestrian activity at annual camp.

Donald Freeth closest to the camera at an Armistice Day parade in Swindon during the inter-war period.

A photograph that reveals the very strong family links within the regiment. SSM Northover, SQMS R. G. N. Sutcliffe, Sgt Wilfred Freeth, Sgt W. H. Haynes, SSM M. Tilley, Capt. A. B. P. L. Vincent 3rd/6th DG (Adjutant), Lt-Col. Mann, RSM S. B. Haines, Sgt Donald Freeth, Sgt Hubert Freeth, and Sgt A. Haynes.

Maj. Lord Ashley, Capt. Viscount Weymouth, and Lt the Earl Cadogan at Corfe Castle in 1934.

The officers at Wilton Park in May 1935, the year of the Silver Jubilee of King George V. *Standing:* Lt P. G. Ormrod, Lt F. A. G. Blackwood, Capt. O. St. M. Thynne, Lt J. G. Morrison, Lt C. H. Fuller, Lt Viscount Weymouth, Lt E. F. Spicer, Lt the Hon. A. E. G. Herbert, Capt. Lord Ashley, Lt H. G. Awdry, Capt. A. M. Gibb, Lt C. E. Awdry, Capt. A. T. Fripp (RAMC), and Capt. M. Bridgeman (RAVC). *Sitting:* Maj. R. E. Vine, Maj. D. G. Williams, Maj. H. J. Nicholson, Maj. A. A. Bankier, Maj. Gen. Blakiston-Houston, Lt-Col. E. P. Awdry, Brig. F. B. Hurndall, Capt. G. L. Welstead (adjutant), Rev. J. J. O'Malley, Maj. S. C. Dumbreck (Brigade Major), and Maj. C. L. Reid. The regiment was inspected by Maj.-Gen. J. M. Blakiston-Houston CB DSO, the inspector general of cavalry, a forthright Ulsterman who had served with the 11th Hussars (PAO) and the mounted infantry in South Africa and was suitably impressed by the yeomen he encountered.

The regimental medical officer in gleaming riding boots attending an injured trooper assisted by Sergeant-Major Norman.

Sergeant-Major Nigel Keevil Carter leading the Malmesbury troop from 'C' Squadron on the dappled grey. He would not survive the war, dying of 'DNBI' disease non-battle injury in Palestine in 1940.

The regimental shooting team. In 1931, marksmanship was at its peak when a 'B' Squadron team won the Yeomanry Challenge Cup for the second year running at the national rifle association meeting at Bisley.

Chilcombe Camp near Winchester in 1936—Maj. S. C. Dumbreck (Brigade Major), Capt. F. F. B. St. George (adjutant), Lt-Col. E. P. Awdry, and RSM Frost.

Arms inspection by Lord Ashley. (*With kind permission of Horsepower, the museum of The King's Royal Hussars*)

Lord Weymouth at the water trough Chilcombe camp. Ken Batt recalled an incident at annual camp in 1939 when the viscount, who was described as rather strict, appeared for morning stables wearing pale blue pyjamas, riding boots, and a cavalry cloak. The yeomen were in awe of any officer who would appear for duty in his pyjamas. (*With kind permission of Horsepower, the museum of The King's Royal Hussars*)

Above: Lord Ashley was the eldest son and heir of the earl of Shaftsbury, whose seat is St Giles House in Dorset. He married Sylvia Hawkes in 1927, a lingerie model and chorus girl described by Tatler, quite possibly with some irony, as 'a charming personality on our stage'. The marriage rather shocked London society at the time, and they were divorced in 1934. She subsequently married a further four times, including a Georgian prince and the Hollywood superstars Douglas Fairbanks senior and Clark Gable. (*Images © National Portrait Gallery London*)

Below: The coronation party for HM King George VI, May 1937. (*With kind permission of Horsepower, the museum of The King's Royal Hussars*)

John Brown's unpublished diary of annual camp in Wimborne St Giles in 1937, which has been transcribed by his daughter and edited by the author, describes the rather relaxed tempo of a pre-war yeomanry camp; this was confirmed by the author's interview with Ken Batt, who described it as 'like a holiday; well better than a holiday'. Lieutenant Brown was allocated the Warminster troop, Lord Weymouth's old troop, and he reports 'a very good one'.

> 30th August: Reveille at 6.00, roll call at 6.15, stables at 6.30; a good-looking lot of men but fair horses.
>
> 31st August: We practised dismounted action and troop drill in open country and not much on in the afternoon so went for a bath at St Giles and met the French Lady Ashley (Francoise Soulier, Lord Ashley's second wife), painted and with a comic dog, a black Kerry Blue bitch puppy.
>
> 1st September: the morning was spent planning for the large manoeuvres and following an early lunch, the Regiment paraded at 12.30ish and moved through St Giles to Wilton where we bivouacked in the drizzle. The men had their dinners and were off about seven and we had conferences and plans to prepare so got in at about 11.
>
> Thursday 2nd September: Up at 2 a.m., paraded at 4 and off at 4.20, the Warminster troop acting as the advanced guard to the column consisting of A Squadron and three batteries of guns moving up the Avon Valley. I put Corporal Arnold's section in front and they did the job very well. It was pitch dark but day began to dawn as we moved down to the valley over the Devizes road. The Avon Valley was most lovely and we went through Wilsford, all fresh and dewy. We spent the whole day at crossings with spells in the bar of the George Hotel, officers in the public bar and men in the private bar. We moved on at 7 to Bulford with lines (horse lines) down in deep long grass. The men had bad grub too.
>
> Saturday 5th September: Morning stables then rifle and sword inspection and pay and bounty all round but had to recall some bounty owing to errors in payment. Then borrowed a car and home for tea. Back to the mess after a bath for a guest night with some not very exciting guests although it cheered up later and got to bed at 2.30
>
> Monday and Tuesday 6th and 7th September: We rode over the hills to Coombe Bissett; the country was very jolly and we watered the horses and fed ourselves, moving off at 2.30 to fight homewards. We were advance guard in the centre and had an impossible task along the main road. We were held up by machine guns and failed to outflank and got properly shot up eventually withdrawing and riding on.

Brown describes the 'A' Squadron parade the next morning with some words of appreciation and criticism from Oliver Thynne (the squadron leader):

> Ferris took me aside (the Adjutant) and told me things were not quite as they should be and I was stepping on the troop's toes. He was most nice, a very good soldier and extremely kind. Conference at 4, in which my exploit down the main road came in for particularly severe criticism.

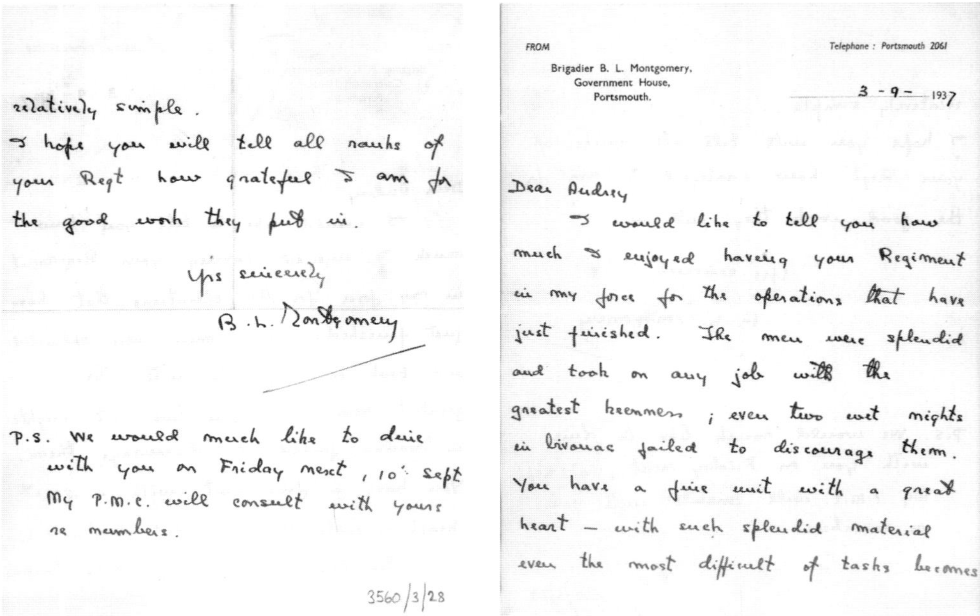

FROM

Brigadier B. L. Montgomery,
Government House,
Portsmouth.

Telephone : Portsmouth 2061

3 - 9 - 1937

Dear Audrey

I would like to tell you how much I enjoyed having your Regiment in my force for the operations that have just finished. The men were splendid and took on any job with the greatest keenness; even two wet nights in bivouac failed to discourage them. You have a fine unit with a great heart – with such splendid material even the most difficult of tasks becomes relatively simple.

I hope you will tell all ranks of your Regt how grateful I am for the good work they put in.

Yrs sincerely

B. L. Montgomery

P.S. We would much like to dine with you on Friday next, 10 Sept. My P.M.C. will consult with yours re numbers.

3560/3/28

Brigadier Bernard Montgomery's letter to the CO following annual training in 1937, which for the first time involved acting as divisional cavalry for a regular formation. Montgomery was a forward-thinking senior officer and saw little use for the mounted soldier.

SSM Carter demonstrating mounted skill at arms in 1937. (*With kind permission of Horsepower, the museum of The King's Royal Hussars*)

'A' Squadron advance to contact at the gallop.

'B' Squadron at Wimborne, St Giles, in September 1937. *Left to right*: Lt C. E. Awdry, Maj. P. W. Pitt, and Capt. A. M. Gibb. This annual training period exposed the yeomen to a variety of weather conditions, but one wonders now, when Germany was investing in armour, battleships, and aircraft, why mounted warfare was seen as a reality in anything other than colonial war fighting.

'Pay correct, Sir.' Lord Ashley at the pay table, 1937. (*With kind permission of Horsepower, the museum of The King's Royal Hussars*)

Tpr Stanley Williams from Swindon at Muntham Court Camp near Worthing, in 1938.
This era of horsed cavalry must have seemed very distant when, four years later, he was a weary and battle-hardened tank commander. The flexibility required from individuals who trained on horses but later fought in tanks has to be admired.

The officers at Muntham Court Camp, Findon, Sussex in 1938. *Standing:* Capt. M. Bridgeman RAVC, Lt H. Blount, Lt H. G. Awdry, Lt and QM F. A. Riddiford, Lt E. F. Spicer, Lt J. G. Morrison, Lt the Hon. A. E. G. Herbert, Lt F. A. G. Blackwood, Lt J. F. Brown, Lt the Earl Cadogan, and Capt. C. L. Broomhead RAMC. *Seated:* Lt C. H. F. Fuller, Lt C. E. Awdry, Capt. Lord Ashley, Capt. O. St. M. Thynne, Lt-Col. H. J. Nicholson MC TD, Col. the Marquess of Bath KG, CB, TD, Col. U. O. Thynne CMG DSO TD, Maj. D. G. Williams, Maj. P. W. Pitt, Capt. and Adjutant F. F. B. St George LG, and Lt Viscount Weymouth.

Lts Blount and Gibb lead the Malmesbury troop during a regimental parade in 1939.

Corfe Castle, 1939. *Standing:* Lt H. G. Awdry, Capt. M. Evans RAMC, Lt F. A. Riddiford QM, Lt G. Best, Lt E. Spicer, Lt Sir J. Clark Bt, Lt M. St J. V. Gibbs, Lt S. V. Christie-Miller, Lt J. Gibb, Lt H. Hunloke, Lt the Earl Cadogan, and Lt J. Brown. *Seated:* Lt F. A. G. Blackwood, Lt J. G. Morrison, Capt. C. E. Awdry, Capt. A. M. Gibb, Maj. P. W. Pitt, Maj. D. G. Williams, Lt-Col. H. Nicholson, Maj. O. Thynne, Maj. Lord Ashley, Capt. Viscount Weymouth, Lt H. Blount, Lt C. Fuller, Lt the Hon. A. E. G. Herbert, Lt the Marquess of Lansdowne, Mr Astley Corbett, Lt C. Thursfield, and Lt W. J. Ewart. This important officers' mess photograph from the last annual camp before mobilisation again illustrates the significant number of influential and powerful Englishmen in the RWY at this time.

Viscount Weymouth, following a busy and rather late night in the mess, awoke in a panic unable to move his legs and was convinced he was paralysed until a fellow officer uncrossed his spurs from his boots he had worn to bed. Many of the wealthy and aristocratic families of the county are represented; both John Morrison and Henry Hunloke were MPs. Two of the British Army's finest senior officers who would feature in the Middle Eastern campaign visited the camp—Lt General Wavell and Brigadier Joe Kingstone, under whom the RWY would serve in Iraq. Lt Blount acted as adjutant for what would be the last peacetime camp.

Lt the Marquess of Lansdowne at attention, with Maj. D. G. Williams and Maj. Lord Ashley. Lt-Col. H. Nicholson MC, who took over as CO in January 1938, handed the regiment over to Maj. Williams in October 1939, who would take it overseas.

Above left: Lt E. Spicer, Lt M. Gibbs, Lt the Earl Cadogan, Lt the Marquess of Lansdowne, and Maj. Lord Ashley. Lord Ashley was later rebadged to the 10th Hussars and served in GHQ Liaison Regiment in north-west Europe. Lt Spicer went on to serve with distinction with the Long Range Desert Group in the Second World War, commanding one of the yeomanry patrols.

Above right: John Brown was educated at Eton and Balliol, working for the Guinness Brewery in Dublin prior to mobilisation. He served in North Africa but was then seconded to the 2nd Rifle Brigade. In December 1944, he lost a leg and was awarded a DSO following a company attack on the formidable hilltop town of Tossignano in the Italian Apennines, which probably needed a brigade to be successful. He returned to brewing after the war and died in 2007 aged ninety-three.

Lieutenant John Brown's diary, which covered this last camp before the war, describes the daily routine of stables, parades, sword drill, lectures on the Bren Gun, lunch, and singing late at night in the mess; however, being that of a carefree young man, it does not mention the changing political situation in Europe.

When the author interviewed Trooper Kenneth Batt in December 2018, he was asked specifically about this time and recalled with complete clarity the fact that many of the yeomen did not believe a war was imminent.

Corporal Cyril Geoffrey Brain, in a recorded interview with the Imperial War Museum, was on the staff of Lloyds Bank in Salisbury before the war and joined the regiment in 1936, his reason for enlistment being his outrage by Adolf Hitler and particularly the treatment of the Jews.

He described the approach to training pre-war as 'somewhat light hearted and certainly never intense'. As an NCO, when war was declared, he supervised the drawing of kit at RHQ in Trowbridge, and like many, he described Wincanton as 'a dreadful place, sleeping under the stands and in the Tote with mud up to the horses' knees'.

Three weeks with the Royal Scots Greys qualified him as a rough-rider corporal, but shortly afterwards, he applied for a commission and joined his brother in the

Wiltshire Regiment despite protests from his friends in the RWY, who reminded him of the short life expectancy of an infantry subaltern in the Great War; 'the fellows said that horses were a form of life insurance as they would not be used in modern warfare.' Brain recalled in his interview that most of these fellows lost their lives.

Later in the war, following an unusual interview at Booths Club in London, he became a Phantom officer joining a troop of this special reconnaissance unit (GHQ Liaison Regiment) that was previously commanded by the actor David Niven.

The last mounted of the RWY parade prior to mobilisation.

5

Mobilisation and the Middle Eastern Adventure

The order to mobilise was received at 3 p.m. on 2 September 1939, the day before war was declared on Germany. Key personnel who could help with the mobilisation process were the first to be called forward, including Corporal Heath (an ex-regular royal horse artilleryman who recalled some of the younger soldiers' mothers hanging onto their arms to avoid them leaving home). Many of these very young troopers had originally enlisted underage and some would eventually be returned from Palestine.

Two days later, the regiment—with a strength of thirty-six officers and 628 men—was formed up at Wincanton racecourse in Somerset, billeted in schools, churches, public houses, and skittle alleys. Many yeomen found themselves sleeping on bare concrete with only army issue blankets to keep out the cold, which, to some, was rather a shock after the comforts of home. Trenches were dug and individuals dispersed to equitation and gas courses before the first batch of horses arrived on the 11th.

Throughout October and November, conditions worsened with knee-deep mud and an outbreak of strangles and catarrh among the horses, limiting any further movement. The regiment had doubled in size six months before and roughly a third of the men were unable to ride, hence Wincanton racecourse was littered with injured riders and bolting horses.

However, worse was to come with a move to a damp and cold Nottinghamshire as the RWY took their place with pride in the 1st Cavalry Division, the last mounted division in the British Army.

The move via rail to Southampton commenced on 5 February 1940 and then onwards to Cherbourg continuing by train to Marseille. The regimental war diary describes 'quite a comfortable day', but this was certainly not the case for some of the troopers sharing unheated wagons with their mounts. On St Valentine's Day 1940, the RWY on board the ship MV *Devonshire* left Marseille for Haifa in Palestine.

'B' Squadron at Rollestone racecourse in the Southwell area of Nottingham, December 1939.

Instability in the Middle East is not a new phenomenon, and Palestine had at times been home to two British divisions, garrisoned there as a regional stabilisation force. The destination was the very comfortable Peninsular Barracks cantonment in the modern town of Haifa, described by the *padre* as 'a cross between Hollywood and the Ideal Home exhibition'.

In March, they moved by rail and then 12 miles by road to a tented camp at Nathanya, a pleasant seaside resort modelling itself on the Riviera with half a dozen hotels, some shops, and a concrete esplanade. Here, the men and horses had three months to acclimatise and enjoyed the relaxed off duty periods.

This somewhat idyllic period did not last long, and when Italy entered the war in June, a move to a hot and desolate Karkur took place where field conditions were much harsher and would provide useful training for the years ahead in the desert.

John Bartholomew was gazetted a second lieutenant in February 1939, following an interview with Colonel Will Fuller of Neston Park. His diary records the excitement of a young man when purchasing his new uniform and 1908 pattern cavalry sword from the regimental tailor Gieves.

Still a student reading economics in Cambridge, he was unable to attend annual camp and instead spent two weeks at the Army School of Equitation at Weedon in Northamptonshire (see image on page 88) being trained by the army show-jumping team, all of whom were later killed in the war.

In August 1939, he was hunting in Northumberland with the Trinity Foot Beagles and returned to London on a train full of 'drunken reservist officers' and then onwards to report to the drill hall in Devizes, where 'B' Squadron was mobilised. He was allocated thirty-five chestnut horses and the Rood Ashton troop, the Marlborough troop having greys, Devizes dark bays, and Melksham light bays. The diaries continue:

> On the 3rd of February we took the 600 odd horses to Rollestone Station and put them into cattle trucks; not an easy task. By now we knew we were bound for Haifa. After a two day stay at Dover due to fog, we embarked the cattle wagons on the train ferry and crossed to Dunkerque. We set off by a French train to cross France having a very pleasant supper interlude at Amiens station with a Guards' battalion and arrived at Marseille on the 8th.
>
> The horses were then led by foot to Chateau Rebars, a distance of sixteen miles, each man leading two horses. The mistral wind blew and it was very cold.

Six days later, the regiment walked back to Marseille and embarked for Palestine. With 800 animals on board the ship, the smell was awful and both men and horses were not at all happy. Bartholomew continues:

> In the end we lost eight horses, most of who had broken legs and were thrown overboard. I had an attack of appendicitis on board but the doctor said he could not operate under such conditions so prescribed complete fasting which cured the problem!

On the day of arrival in Palestine, there was rioting in Haifa and the diarist described purchasing a Swiss automatic pistol with ammunition and instantly felt much safer. The diary then continues in Nathanya:

> A very attractive spot with acres of orange groves and excellent bathing despite the dangerous currents which almost drowned Trooper Waterhouse. With so many racehorses and polo ponies having been bought as remounts, I had a lot of pleasure playing polo and also racing at Sarafand. I had a very useful hurdler called Coral Reef, who I rode second in the Palestine Grand National, being beaten by Bruce Hobbs, who won the 1939 Grand National at Liverpool.

The three months spent near the sea allowed the men and horses time to acclimatise with plenty of sea bathing for the yeomen and their mounts. Polo was played, gymkhanas and mule racing kept the troops riding fit, and some of the officers' wives even made the journey out from England. Despite these pleasures, there was an undercurrent of unease among the yeomen as they heard stories of the misery in northern France and at home. The temperature had risen significantly by May when troop and then squadron training started in earnest.

Lt F. A. Riddiford, the quartermaster, was born in 1891 in Portsea, Hampshire. He served in the First World War with the 21st (Empress of India's) Lancers. He was clearly a talented soldier as his progression through the ranks was remarkably rapid given the nature of a peacetime army. An expert horseman, when he was married in Saugor, Bengal Province in 1920, the marriage register gives his profession as 'Rough Rider, 21st Lancers'.

He transferred to the Royal Tank Corps in 1919 and later moved to the 16th/5th the Queen's Royal Lancers, where he was promoted to sergeant-major in 1924 and later RSM. Riddiford's passion was photography, so much so that he applied to be an army photographer and thankfully was turned down as he was later commissioned in 1935 as a lieutenant in the RWY, promoted substantive captain in October 1941; temporary major in 1942; and major in 1947.

Many of the images in this chapter originated from negatives from his photographic collection. In the 1960s, he still attended annual camp and organised the administration for the officers' mess—a truly remarkable cavalryman.

2Lt John 'Boy' Bartholomew.

Bronzed, relaxed, and apparently carefree Royal Wiltshire Yeomen peeling potatoes in Palestine.

Exercising the regiment's horses on the beach at Nathanya.

Above left: Capt. Blount, Capt. St George (the adjutant from the Life Guards), and Maj. Thynne all impeccably attired, off duty but carrying sidearms in spring 1940. In May 1941, the adjutant was posted to the Middle Eastern Cavalry School and Capt. the Earl Cadogan (who had previously served as a regular officer in the Coldstream Guards) took up the position.

Above right: Capt. Rev. L. A. Fereday, originally a Cornish vicar, enlisted at the outbreak of war. The *padre* was a popular officer and another keen photographer who organised trips to nearby Jerusalem and Galilee. He served with the RWY until 1943 when ill health forced his return home, but he continued to serve in the Territorial Army after the war, leaving in 1956 as a chaplain fourth class.

Lt-Col. D. G. Williams was promoted to commanding officer in October 1939, his tour coming to an end in March 1941. He was replaced by a regular officer experienced in tank warfare and was greatly missed by his regiment.

Above: A sight familiar to yeomen throughout the generations—the influential quartermaster and his team. The QM was invariably commissioned as a senior NCO and was highly respected by both officers and men.

Below left: The regimental second in command, Maj. Oliver Thynne, in an unusual order of dress, even by yeomanry standards where dress regulations have always been viewed as a guide rather than a rule. The son of a previous commanding officer, Oliver Thynne, joined 'A' Squadron at Warminster in 1920. He was posted to a staff appointment in the Middle East Intelligence Centre in Cairo in 1942 and worked with the mysterious 30 Committee, who were responsible for managing double agents in the Middle East. He would eventually be promoted to lieutenant-colonel.

Below right: Maj. Alistair Gibb, who would go on to command the regiment between 1942 and 1944 and in the post-war years became honorary colonel. Born in 1901, he was educated at Eton and Oxford and worked for the family firm of engineers. He was a keen polo player and related in his second marriage to Lord Cowdray, who he helped with the revival of polo at Cowdray Park in West Sussex and was later president of Cirencester Park Polo Club. He had a house in the Happy Valley region of Kenya where he also played polo, but he died tragically in a polo accident during Goodwood week at Cowdray in the summer of 1955.

The officers' batmen. The term soldier servant or valet was replaced by 'batman' in the inter-war years. This was a desirable position, as looking after an officer, his uniform, and his kit was certainly a less onerous task than many other squadron duties. (*From the collection of Trooper Williams, first row fifth from the right*)

Above left: Tpr Ted Bolton, whose life is covered later in the book, mounted on Blanco.

Above right: Tpr Ford in Nathanya.

Right: L/Cpl Davis manning an obsolete Hotchkiss machine gun. A French machine gun designed by an Austrian but altered by a Coventry factory to take the British .303 round, the Hotchkiss was one of the first air-cooled heavy machine guns but as would be discovered later in Syria, it was not particularly useful in the anti-aircraft role. A large number of these weapons were discovered in store in Palestine, possibly left over from the previous war.

Below: Tprs Ron Williams and Les Smart.

The relaxed and rather pleasant life in Nathanya in the spring of 1940.

South-east of Haifa, Mount Carmel and the Carmel Range was a popular tourist destination, full of biblical and military history including the battle of Megiddo during the Palestine campaign of the First World War.

The subject of these officers' intense concentration is clearly four-legged.

Above: Life off duty was very similar to peacetime colonial soldiering as these images from L/Cpl Davies's collection demonstrate. In England, the Cavalry Division in Palestine had been rather cruelly named 'the Palestine Home Guard'. The unnamed trooper in the picture appears to have either a cover over his service dress hat or a privately purchased tropical version.

Opposite page: Regimental Medical Officer Capt. Morgan Evans and the family of the baby he delivered. Born in Llanharan, Wales, he entered Llandovrey sixth form at the very young age of fourteen; in addition to his academic prowess, he was also an extremely talented rugby player. He studied medicine at Oxford and the Middlesex Hospital Medical School in London, graduating in 1933; while a student, he played for London Welsh.

Well-read and a hunting and shooting man, he took up his post as a GP in Chippenham; when asked why, his response was 'it had to be the Quorn or the Beaufort, and the Beaufort was nearer Wales.' He joined the regiment in 1935, leaving to command a field ambulance and served throughout the war receiving an MBE. A man of great depth and humour, he rejoined his beloved regiment post-war, eventually retiring in 1963. His son, a consultant anaesthetist, served in the RAMC in the First Gulf War.

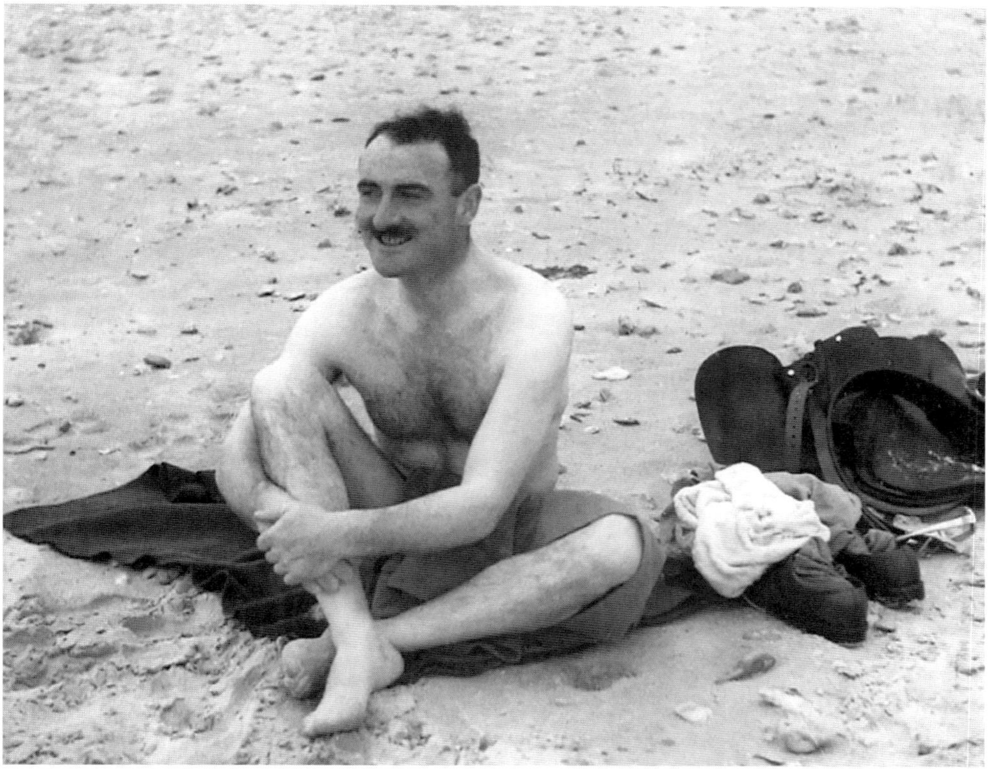

Maj. M. Bridgman RAVC, the veterinary officer.

A sight that would worry many yeomen—a group of officers with a map. The medical officer is far right of picture.

Above: Tpr Denis Strachan from 'C' Squadron wearing a uniform that would have been familiar to yeomen during the First World War.

Right: The shooters: Lt-Col. D. Williams, Capt. the Earl Cadogan, and Lt C. Fuller watched by Lt the Hon. A. Herbert.

The funeral of Tpr Walter Haywood (405153), Haifa War Cemetery, 1940. The son of John and Lucy Haywood of Nottingham, and husband of Joyce, he died on 22 July 1940 aged only twenty-eight. His headstone carries the inscription: 'In memory's garden we meet every day. Loving wife and daughter.'

SSM Tulk and SQMS Salisbury enjoying a picnic at Kfar Yona, 7 km east of Nathanya. Tulk was mobilised in August 1939 and as a sergeant was part of the advance party sent to Palestine to take over the camp. Salisbury was mobilised as a corporal from 'A' Squadron, promoted in 1940, and went on to become RQMS, leaving the regiment in January 1943 to take up a QM commission.

In his very personal account of life in the regiment during the Second World War (which was privately published in 1993), Mick Collins describes:

> A favourite ploy employed by some of the more knowledgeable troopers out on a manoeuvre was, if a horse cast a shoe just before moving off was not to report the fact but to secrete the cast shoe in their tunic. Once the troop was some distance out the cast shoe would be surreptitiously dropped in the tracks where it would be spotted by the sharp-eyed NCO bringing up the rear. Then the NCO would yell out, 'inspect your horses feet' and an innocent looking trooper would fall out and return to camp, thereafter enjoying smoking while riding, raiding orange groves, and chasing imaginary foxes.

On 3 October, there was a further short move of RHQ, HQ, and 'B' Squadrons to Hadera Sea Camp, with 'A' Squadron remaining in billets in the small town of Hadera itself. 'C' Squadron was detached, undertaking searchlight duties in Egypt, and two weeks later, the regiment was further fragmented as 'B' Squadron also departed for searchlight training. Little activity is recorded in the war diary, other than some low-level exercises against the Warwickshire Yeomanry and the slow and rather tedious pace of life continued.

Lt Kenneth Mcillwraith, who will appear later in the story of the Battle of Palmyra, departed for service with 51 (Middle Eastern) Commando for a short period of time, reappearing back at regimental duty two months later at his own request.

There was, however, a degree of excitement when the well-known film star, amateur jockey, and old Etonian Charles (Teddy) Underdown, who had been serving as a sergeant in the regiment, was granted a commission in November. His initial approach to the RWY had proved unsuccessful when he listed his occupation as 'film star'—possibly the ultimate gentleman ranker who in later life would have roles in movies as diverse as *Thunderball* and *Tarka the Otter*.

As the spring of 1940 progressed, the holiday atmosphere increased as several of the officers' wives arrived from England, but as May brought news of military disasters at home, the mood became sombre and activity was refocused on military training. On 5 June, when the weather was oppressively hot, the regiment started the move from Nathanya, 20 miles inland, to Karkur, a British camp recently vacated by a fellow yeomanry regiment the Yorkshire Dragoons. The ground was very hard, which affected the horses, some becoming quite lame and the soldiers were now exposed to the rural Middle East for the first time and more importantly the health hazards of sandfly fever and jaundice.

Right: SQMS Pike of 'A' Squadron with Tpr Spender and Sgt Locke, the RWY turf accountants during the popular pastime of mule racing. In April 1940, equestrian activity increased as the 1st Remount Squadron arrived from England with 700 horses, which allowed polo to be played twice a week. Mule racing kept the soldiers entertained.

Below: The *padre* with the locally contracted barber.

Left: Digging in at Karkur.

Below: 'A' Squadron Guard, Karkur, 1940. Regimental training with horses continued, and in July 1940, the RWY exercised for the last time as a complete mounted regiment; early in August, 'C' Squadron left for Egypt to re-role as an anti-aircraft searchlight unit.

The CO leading the regiment out from the camp on a field exercise.

Officers in typical desert attire.

Gambling on scorpion fighting. Karkur was desolate and led to boredom, which has always been the enemy of officers and NCOs throughout the history of any army; restless soldiers can find other ways to amuse themselves. There were many volunteers for elite airborne and commando units, but few were chosen.

The last full mounted parade of the RWY at Karkur. During the time spent at Karkur, the regiment was informed to its great disappointment that it was to be converted into a searchlight unit, a role normally performed by the Royal Artillery. The last full regimental parade was not as ordered as the photograph implies.

Tpr Stan Williams, bare-headed in the Mus Mus pass outside Karkur.

Maj. Thynne leading HQ and 'A' Squadron on Christmas Day 1940. The CO had been in Egypt for two weeks, where he had been arranging for 'B' Squadron under Capt. Awdry to relieve 'C' Squadron under Maj. Gibb in the western desert, although he managed to return in time for the important morale boost of Christmas dinner served in the local cinema.

An officers *v.* sergeants football match at Hadera Sea Camp, 1940. Wearing a blazer is Jim Paviour, the ex-English amateur international footballer who acted as the referee. He arrived in Palestine as a reinforcement in the autumn of 1940. After the war, he became player manager for Trowbridge Town and was landlord of the Lamb Inn in Mortimer Street. On his left is Maj. Viscount Weymouth of Longleat. Sgt Les Townsend of HQ Squadron, also from Trowbridge, is pictured third from right in the middle row. RSM Frost is extreme right and Maj. Morgan Evans, the medical officer, is shown third left in the front row. The final score was officers two to sergeants three.

An Uncomfortable Distraction with Searchlights

In August 1940, 'C' Squadron was dispatched to Egypt to start searchlight duty as a deterrent against Italian air raids on North African ports. The simple reason why the yeomen was that they were available and there was an acute shortage of trained Royal Artillery searchlight crew in the Middle East.

'B' relieved 'C' Squadron in November, who were immediately tasked with protecting the small but important Egyptian port of Sollum on the Libyan border. Following a rather miserable Christmas with sandstorms, heavy bombing, and a 'most truculent Commanding officer from the Argyll and Sutherland Highlanders', who objected to the disturbance caused by the RWY searchlights, a detachment of four lights was sent forwards to Tobruk with others later sent to Benghazi.

Reinforcements and supplies made the hazardous journey from the railhead at Mersah Matruh until Tobruk was surrounded by the enemy following a rapid Allied withdrawal towards Egypt. The RWY was therefore present for three months at the siege of Tobruk from April 1941, leaving on HMAS *Stuart* for Cairo in June 1941, finally rejoining the regiment in Aleppo in August.

Motorisation and the gradual loss of horses started in January 1941 following a move to a hutted camp at Jenin situated on the disused Baghdad railway.

'C' Squadron in Alexandria undergoing searchlight training.

A sight familiar to many soldiers throughout the ages—the acquisition of a tattoo. During the author's service, the Prince of Wales feathers and the fern leaf has been inked onto the legs and buttocks of both officers and soldiers in varying parts of the world.

This was a sad day following 150 years as horsed cavalry, but over the next three months, the challenge of fighting from the 15-cwt Morris truck was accepted with enthusiasm.

Some 50 km south of Haifa, Jenin had in the late 1930s become a centre for the rebellion against the British presence in Palestine and the Cavalry Division's role was primarily to protect Northern Palestine against the perceived threat from Vichy-occupied Syria but also as a deterrent to drug smugglers.

Captain the Earl Cadogan recorded the 'filthy state of the entire area caused by the carelessness of the previous units'. 'C' Squadron was the first to start mechanisation, and de-horsing started at the end of February. By early March, only thirty horses remained, with a further thirty-eight destined for the Greek Army.

In an interview with a relative, the author was told of the great sadness when it became apparent that these horses would probably be slaughtered for meat.

In 1941, as now, the situation in Iraq was unstable; the Arabs were convinced that Britain had no future in the Middle East and the political situation worsened in March 1941 as a new pro-German prime minister took control of the country and (possibly, more importantly) the oil reserves.

By 1 April, the regiment (less 'B' Squadron, who were still in Tobruk) was established in the hill town of Nablus albeit rather scattered between an excellent fort just outside on the Jerusalem road and billets in the town itself. The usual round of brigade and divisional staff officers visited, and on 8 May, orders were received to move to Irbid in Transjordan.

An impeccably turned out RSM Frost at Jenin, still dressed for the saddle.

The signal troop football team, with Tpr Hanney far right of the picture.

Garages are the new stables in Jenin.

The 1st Cavalry Division commanded by Major-General John Clark was now called to help and the regiment together with the Household Cavalry Regiment, and the Warwickshire Yeomanry formed the mounted element to the newly created HABFORCE. The formation acquired the name KINGCOL, after Brigadier Joe Kingstone, a cavalryman who served with the Queen's Bays (2nd Dragoon Guards) and later commanded the 9th Queen's Royal Lancers; in 1941, he was rumoured to be the best fighting brigadier in the British Army.

Captain Thursfield (shown in the 1939 officers' photograph) was appointed to the brigade staff as signals officer, an important task with the vast and inhospitable terrain of the Iraqi desert. Logistical problems were significant with over 100 of the regiment left at Nablus due to a lack of transport.

The RWY started on their somewhat chaotic and uncomfortable journey on 12 May, spending a very unpleasant two weeks in the desert guarding the oil pipeline. The route to the besieged Allied garrison at Habbaniya in Iraq (sixty years later, Major Richard Morgan, 'B' (RWY) Squadron RWxY also served here) involved a series of landmarks H1–4, interspersed at intervals of between 70 and 100 miles, which were well-equipped pumping stations along the vital pipeline from Kirkuk to Haifa.

As the spring turned to early summer and the temperature climbed, news arrived from Tobruk of the first death of a Wiltshire yeoman in action. The patrols in the Iraqi desert continued interspersed by occasional air raids from Vichy French planes until 20 June when the regiment was moved four miles from the Syrian frontier.

The RWY *padre* at an oil well in Iraq 1941.

Right: Tprs Legge and Gambles from HQ Squadron setting up another temporary home in yet another desert (Green Parrot H4).

Below: Cpl Davis at 'H4' on the Trans-Jordan Pipeline in the Iraq desert 1941. The task was to guard divisional headquarters and its lines of communication; the conditions were appalling with one of the worst hot desert winds for many years as demonstrated by these miserable and fatigued yeomen.

During the advance to Habbaniya, the Arab Legion under the command of Maj. John Bagot Glubb (Glubb Pasha), originally a Royal Engineer, remained the only Arab unit loyal to the Allies. With long hair and dressed in flowing robes, armed with a variety of knives and weapons, they became known as Glubb's Girls.

Lt the Marquess of Lansdowne's troop was the first to arrive in Habbaniya on 27 May. The RAF station was one of the most impressive in the Empire and the yeomanry officers above are clearly engrossed by the lineage of the Royal Exodus Hunt pack, an unusual organisation in the hunting world as it was run by the RAF. The original image is labelled left to right: Capt. the Earl Cadogan, Lt Jimmy James, Nigel (unidentified officer), Lt Peter Lawson, an Iraqi Levee officer, and Lt the Hon. A. Herbert.

The Campaign in Syria (Operation Exporter)

The next Middle Eastern country on the undesirable list was Syria, which, like Iraq and Persia, was under the influence of Germany and garrisoned by the hated Vichy French. The strategic concern was that Syria could be utilised by the Axis forces to mount attacks on Egypt.

The RWY (less one squadron) was part of the 4th Cavalry Brigade and, again with the Household Cavalry and the Warwickshire Yeomanry, were given the objective of the ancient and ruined city of Palmyra, 100 miles from the Iraq border.

On 21 June 1941, the CO, Lt-Col. Williams, led the advance, which was joined by a company of the Arab Legion, reaching Juffa (50 miles inside Syria), where a lone French aircraft escaped to warn the main Vichy garrisons at Homs and Palmyra.

Arriving at the outskirts of Palmyra at 11 a.m., the CO briefed his squadrons overlooking the ruined city and the objective of Yellow Ridge (the most prominent landmark occupied by dug-in French machine guns). With no air support or artillery, numerous foot patrols were sent forward, but progress was painfully slow against such a well-prepared enemy.

Sheltering in slit trenches and suffering in the intense heat for twelve days, the regiment's vehicles were systematically destroyed. The relentless Vichy bombing attacks that followed from the air were difficult to counter with rifles and old Hotchkiss machine guns.

Lt M. St J. V. Gibbs distinguished himself by assaulting the hills but had to withdraw due to a combination of exhaustion and overwhelming opposition. Trooper Ken Batt in an interview with the author recalled his orders from Sergeant Bannister 'get up that hill and if you see anyone in front of you, shoot them'.

Lieutenant Kenneth Mcllwraith, the Canadian-born liaison officer, was tasked to take a French prisoner back to Brigade HQ, but his car was attacked, and he and his batman were taken prisoner on 2 June by a French patrol. He was handed over to a French Foreign Legion officer and flown 145 km to Homs in an ancient biplane whose Gallic pilot was far more concerned with the cases of wine he was transferring than the welfare of his prisoners. From Homs, he was flown to Greece and then onwards to Salonika. The conditions in which he and other British prisoners were held in a dockside warehouse were appalling, but after five days, he was moved to a passenger ship.

Following the armistice between the British and Vichy forces on 14 July, Mcllwraith was transported through Germany to Toulon in southern France, again in horrific conditions, and finally by sea to Beirut and Cairo. He rejoined the regiment but missed the Battle of El Alamein due to jaundice and desert sores; the crewman who replaced him was killed in the battle. Mcllwraith was clearly traumatised by these experiences because he rarely spoke about them after the war.

Returning to the battle unfolding in Syria, by 26 June, the daily bombing and strafing had reduced as the RAF stepped up activity against the French airfields.

Water was now rationed to 1 gallon a day, but thankfully, artillery support had arrived to turn the tide.

Further attacks by RWY patrols and soldiers from the Essex Regiment were made on the prominent ridge overlooking the town and repeatedly repulsed, but on 3 July, the enemy garrison finally surrendered.

He was badly wounded on 23 June 1941. Two weeks later, QM Riddiford wrote to Bath's family:

> Our small convoy of vehicles was attacked by fighters and the driver of the lorry in which your son was riding was killed instantly and all the others were wounded. After the fighter had gone and left us, I saw that your son's vehicle was still travelling and assumed it was all right. Instead, I found that your son, although badly wounded had climbed into the driver's seat and driven the vehicle for nearly a mile. Before we could get the wounded away, we were again attacked.
>
> He had to take himself thirty miles to the nearest dressing station where the doctors who attended him were full of admiration of his courage.

Bath died three days after this action, but when Riddiford wrote to the family, he was clearly unaware of his death. He was posthumously awarded the Military Medal and now lies in Habbaniya War Cemetery in Iraq, 65 km west of Baghdad.

By 29 June 1941, both 'A' and 'C' Squadrons could only muster seventy-eight fit men. Somerset de Chair in his book *The Golden Carpet* described the air bombardment of the RWY:

> South of Palmyra bluff John Morrison of the Wilts, who was to join me in Parliament a year later, told me he had seventeen vehicles under his command on the first

Tpr Eric Llewellyn Bath MM 324515 from Trowbridge.

One of the few photographs in existence showing an RWY patrol under attack from Vichy French aircraft in Syria.

> morning and only four left including the water wagon, the next day; the rest were destroyed by air attack.

The regimental war diary records the whole of 'A' Echelon destroyed by machine gun fire from the air.

Following the fall of Palmyra, the regiment prepared for an attack on Homms, but the Syrian armistice intervened and the yeomen trekked northwards to Aleppo where the 4th Cavalry Brigade was concentrating. They bivouacked in olive groves north-east of the town, where shade following the incessant heat and glare of the desert sun was most welcome, as was the abundance of fresh fruit after a diet made up of bully beef and biscuits for two months. The yeomen were allowed into Aleppo in the evening, which was full of French soldiers—an odd sight as the French Foreign Legion had previously been the despised enemy at Palmyra.

A particularly distasteful incident took place in June 1941 when a patrol from the Warwickshire Yeomanry was approached by vehicles sent from a French fort under the protection of a white flag. Under the command of an Arab officer, the Warwickshires were raked with machine gun fire from trucks and armoured cars. The identity of the Arab Vichy officer is unclear as he is referred to by three different names in first-hand accounts and the published regimental history, but one possibility is the infamous 'Arab Nazi' Fawzi-al-Qawukji.

What is clear to the author from interviewing families is that little quarter was given to the Vichy forces during the final mopping up operations in Palmyra. It was at Aleppo on 4 August that 'B' Squadron rejoined and the regiment was once more united.

Heat exhaustion, flies, and fatigue were an ever-present threat during the Battle of Palmyra fought in the blistering Syrian summer where the temperature can reach 40°C. By 29 June 1941, both 'A' and 'C' Squadrons could only muster seventy-eight fit men.

Above left: SQMS Pike, RQMS Wheeler, and 'Darky' Hale. RQMS Leslie Wheeler was a highly regarded senior NCO, who would be commissioned as QM later in the war and privately published his wartime memoirs in his eighties.

A group of haggard officers after the battle.

Left: Tpr Hare, an unknown soldier, Tpr Gambles, Tpr Powell and Tpr Orsett in Arak, an ancient village 20 miles north of Palmyra in their battle-scarred Ford pick-up truck. Lt-Col. Pitt's regimental history refers to this site as 'Rek' and many of the photographs are labelled as 'Rekke'.

Below: Lt Riddiford, Maj. Awdry, Lt the Earl Cadogan, Maj. Thynne, and Lt-Col. Williams in Aleppo.

Operations in Persia (Operation Countenance)

The importance of transport routes to Russia and the obvious oil pipeline led to this rather overlooked and brief campaign. Persia was another Middle Eastern country that enjoyed a good relationship with Germany, and following a failure of diplomacy, a plan was devised to join hands with the Russian Army via Persia.

On 9 August, the RWY moved 65 miles by road south to Baghdad, where the men were surprisingly allowed a night in the town, and thereafter to the town of Kurkuk where the temperature was seldom below 120 degrees. Bathing in the river was arranged, but this was a 17-mile trip through the desert. Sickness was now commonplace, and at least thirty men were hospitalised with the ever-present threat of sandfly fever.

The Allied advance into Iraq on 26 August was initially led by the Warwickshire Yeomanry with a detachment of the 14th/20th Hussars through treacherous countryside, and the RWY took the lead a few days later. This was not to be a prolonged campaign, and two days later, the RWY was awakened by shellfire, but by 12.30 that day, the Persians had surrendered.

For the first few days of September, reconnaissance patrols were sent out from the area surrounding Kermamshah, midway between Baghdad and Tehran. Of interest to the modern reader is the turbulence and fighting between Persian and Iraqi Kurds and the general inclination of deserters from the Persian Army and local rebels to loot whenever possible. Malaria, smallpox, and typhus were a constant threat, and the troops avoided entering the local towns. On 15 September, the move towards Tehran over dreadfully potholed and corrugated roads started.

The strategic plan was for a simultaneous entry to Tehran by Allied and Soviet forces on 17 September, but the Russians chose to ignore this and led by General Novikov, entered the capital much earlier at 6 a.m.

The route to Persia through the harsh countryside of the Paitak Pass.

A vehicle crew take a rest at the top of the Marble Mountain range in Persia.

Twenty minutes halt after the Battle of Shahbad *en route* to Tehran. Frequently, the population of an entire town would appear to watch the passing yeomen.

The RWY was garrisoned with the Household Cavalry, 'A' Squadron of 13th Lancers, Indian Army, a detachment of 19th Medium Battery Royal Artillery and the 1/5th Gurkha Rifles in a large and new German armament factory where a total of 3,000 troops were billeted in very unsanitary conditions. However, the city was peaceful, and the Russians were found to be surprisingly friendly.

Above, below and opposite: At 11 a.m. on 23 September, a joint parade was held on the square in the factory. Fifteen officers and seventy other ranks from 9th Armoured Brigade formed up on the square facing a similar number of Russians. Following an inspection by the Russian Gen. Novikov and Brigade Commander Brigadier Tiarks, both contingents marched past, three cheers were proposed for both armies, and for some, the party began, helped by an excellent Russian band with songs, dances, and copious amounts of the ubiquitous vodka.

The RWY Are Finally Converted to an Armoured Regiment

The Persian adventure had achieved its aim, stabilising the country and establishing a supply route to Russia for the remainder of the war. On 8 October, having left Tehran twelve days prior, the regiment travelled over 1,375 miles, arriving at Gadera near Tel Aviv, where a week of much-needed leave was awarded to all ranks.

The RWY had now taken part in three separate campaigns fighting from their Peugeot and Morris trucks and more importantly for what was to come, the soldiers had learned to survive in the harsh desert conditions during this 8,000-mile excursion since leaving Palestine. Lieutenant Mcillwraith now rejoined the regiment following his capture at the Battle of Palmyra.

Gadera was where the transition to an armoured regiment took place, but life in this overcrowded camp was not particularly comfortable, and by Christmas, relentless rain had turned the ground into a quagmire of mud with a river running through the camp.

Serge battledress had at least now been issued to the Regiment which significantly improved morale, and by March 1942, they were back at Karkur Road Camp for gunnery practice, albeit with only four tanks.

By early August, when Winston Churchill visited the brigade, tanks were still scarce with only nine Crusaders, one Stuart light tank, and two scout cars held on strength. The prime minister promised a resupply with up-to-date Shermans and the latest Mk 3 Crusaders but was insistent they would be ready for action by October.

By 24 August, a composite regiment with the Warwickshire Yeomanry moved west to Wadi Latrun, but by early September, further reorganisation had taken place as the RWY returned to a single regiment and the eagerly awaited armour started to arrive. The regiment was now part of the 2nd New Zealand Division, and the training was now very focused on the battle to come that would be remembered for evermore as the RWY's finest hour.

Tprs Dunn and Collis at the squadron office, Christmas 1941. Collis was mobilised with HQ Squadron in 1939 and Dunn joined as a reinforcement in the autumn of 1940.

Gadera, 1942. A local boy was paid to do the laundry. Note the Wellington boots on the figure on the right.

Above left: A regimental Christmas card from 1941.

Above right: On 20 March 1942, the commanding officer, Lt-Col. D. G. Williams, having reached the age limit, handed over to Lt-Col. P. T. W. Sykes from the Queen's Bays, who would supervise the transition to the armoured role that would start in earnest in Egypt at Qassasin Camp near Cairo.

Lt Nigel Keevil Carter TD (1907–1942) relaxing off duty prior to his commission. Note the Prince of Wales feathers on his right wrist below his badge of rank.

Son of William and Annie Carter, of Arches Farm, Malmesbury, he was mobilised in 1939 as the popular squadron sergeant-major of ‘C’ Squadron and married later in 1940. He was commissioned on 11 November 1941, but sadly died of sandfly fever and lies in the Ramleh War cemetery outside Tel Aviv. His headstone carries the inscription: ‘There’s some corner of a foreign field that is forever England’. (*Images provided by his nephew David Jones*)

Above: A sergeant of the Melksham Cavalry, *c.* 1800, from an oil painting in the collection of the late John Mollo, an acknowledged expert in the field of military dress.

Right: Malmesbury Troop Sergeant George Butler in August 1818, wearing the Tarleton pattern-crested helmet.

Quartermaster Joseph Moore joined the Chippenham troop in 1794. This portrait was painted in 1835 at the distinguished age of sixty-five and is still displayed in the Army Reserve Centre in Swindon.

Thomas Fraser Grove (1821–1897) above right was born in Ferne, Wiltshire. He served with the 6th (Inniskilling) Dragoons from 1842–1849, selling out as a captain. He sat as a Liberal MP for South Wiltshire and for the Wilton Division; he was made a baronet in 1874. He was clearly a busy man as he served as a deputy lieutenant and justice of the peace for Wiltshire and was high sheriff from 1861–1862.

He was commissioned into the RWY as a cornet, the cavalry term for a subaltern, in 1852, and served in the Chippenham troop, regaining his former army rank of captain in 1856. Promoted to major in 1876, he eventually commanded the regiment until 1888. He holds the blue and silver light dragoon pattern kepi that would later be replaced by a hussar pattern busby.

George Troyte-Bullock wears the uniform of the West Somerset Yeomanry; his son, Lt-Col. Edward Troyte-Bullock, eventually went on to command the Dorset Yeomanry.

An undated watercolour of an officer in 1898, displaying the ornate, silver-embroidered sabretache, which was designed as a document carrier for mounted troops that by virtue of its flat surface could also be used as a writing pad. It evolved into a decorative and very expensive item, but by the early 1900s, it was officially abolished. The RWY sabretache changed with the uniform from a light dragoon design to the splendid hussar pattern shown above. Very few of these are still in existence, but the ornate decoration remains on the table mats used in the officers and SNCO's dining room in Old Sarum Army Reserve Centre. The overalls shown in the image are cut looser than later in the Victorian period and more in the style of the 1870s.

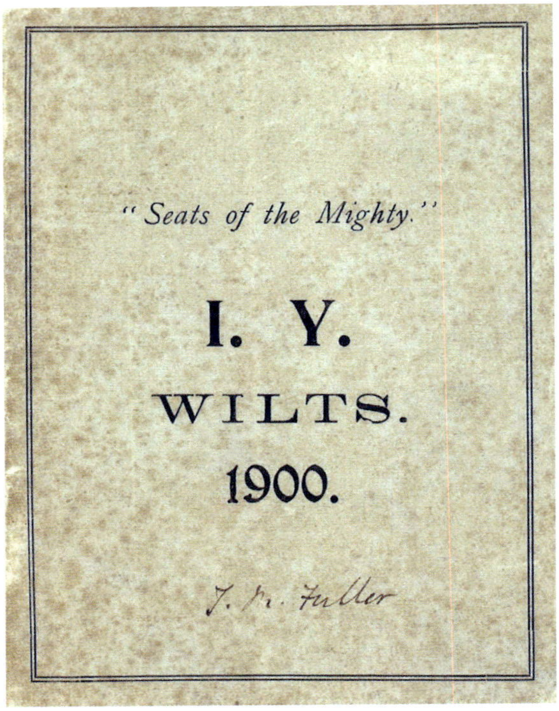

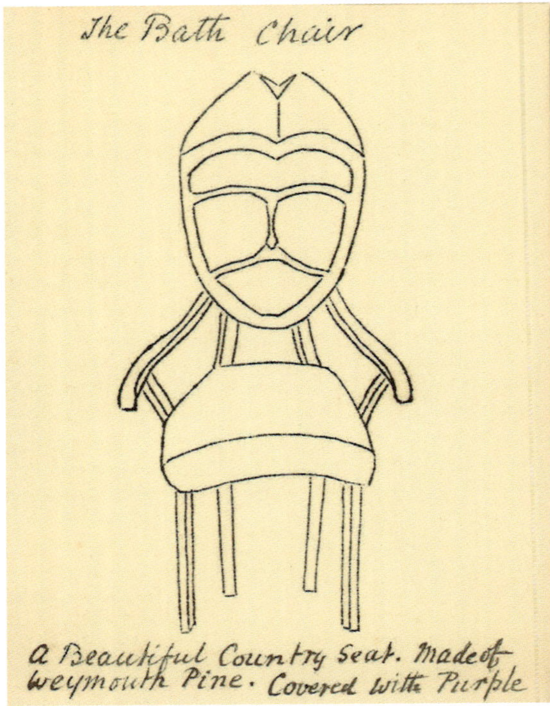

Above: Seats of the Mighty with every apology to *Punch* respectfully dedicated to Colonel the Right Honourable W. H. Long MP as a little memento of the Wilts Imperial Yeomanry by 'Paymaster'. This small booklet depicted the officers as caricatures in the form of carved, wooden dining chairs.

Left: Maj. (later Lt-Col.) Walter Hume Long wearing full dress in 1903.

Right: The artist Caran-Rouge depicted many regiments of the British Army in a similar style to the better-known caricaturist 'Snaffles'. This watercolour and gouache painting from 1911 illustrates the short-lived but elegant Glamorgan blue Egyptian style tunic, a hybrid of full dress and blue patrols. The painting is technically incorrect as the overalls would have had silver stripes and the forage cap had at this time changed. (*Author's collection*)

Below: The Marquess of Ailesbury. (*Images © National Portrait Gallery London and Major John Morgan TD*)

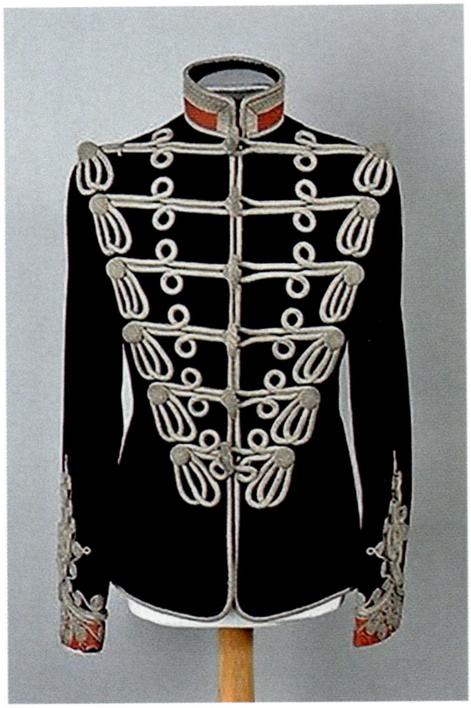

Above left: George Mackay, who served from 1894–1917, was an old Etonian from Holt near Trowbridge and a director of Palmer and Mackay, a well-known cloth mill in the town. He was on parade with a squadron commanded by Lord Bruce when HRH the Prince of Wales visited Cheltenham in 1897.

Above right: Detail of an officer's full dress tunic. (*Major John Morgan TD*)

Below: Edgar Hinton was killed in action in 1918. His brother was a POW and was unaware he was dead.

Above: A Christmas card sent home to Wiltshire in 1916.

Right: Sgt Eric Woodman. Behind the horse lines in Nathanya was an orange grove surrounded by a mimosa hedge—a marvellous combined scent. Oranges were of course incredibly scarce at home.

Anti-tank defences and minefields at El Alamein as depicted by Wilhelm Wessel, Rommel's official war artist. These German minefields contained half a million mines and were 6,000 yards deep in places. (*Image attributed to Stadt Iserlohn Germany*)

David Shepherd's dark but atmospheric oil painting depicting a Crusader tank commanded by Capt. Gibbs overrunning a German 88-mm anti-tank gun approaching the Rahman Track. Some 200 prints were produced, and the original still hangs in the Swindon Army Reserve Centre. (*With thanks to the late David Shepherd's daughter Mandy and the trustees of his estate*)

Above left: An RWY trumpet banner. (*Image courtesy of Bosleys auctioneers*)

Above right: Tpr David Gadd, Castlemartin Ranges on the south Pembrokeshire coast in 1960. He left the Wiltshire Army Cadet Force at sixteen and joined the RWY in 1959. He served for twenty years until 1980 when he was a troop sergeant and D and M instructor.

Daimler armoured car Mark 2 during Exercise Banbury Chase, 1960. The Dingo's big brother first entered service in 1941, seeing action in the North African desert, and was designed to add some fire support to the reconnaissance regiment. With a range of 200 miles and a top speed of 50 mph, in its day, it was considered an advanced design but would be replaced in the early 1960s by the Saladin.

From left to right: No. 1 Guard 'B' Squadron, No. 2 Guard 'C' Squadron, No. 3 Guard HQ Squadron, and No. 4 Guard 'A' Squadron. Lt-Col. Magnall is mounted facing the earl of Pembroke with red stripes on his overalls and Colonel J. G. Morrison on his right on the saluting dais. John King's print of the parade was limited to seventy-five copies. The original oil painting still hangs in the Army Reserve Centre in Swindon, but a little-known watercolour of the same parade by the artist is in the author's collection.

Above left: The guidon of the Royal Wiltshire Yeomanry.

Above right: Gunnery at Lulworth. Cpl David Gadd front left and Tpr David Stevens front centre.

Right: Lulworth Ranges, Dorset, in the 1960s. Note the vehicle commander wearing a forage cap. Lt David Thomas, a keen hunting man who won the inter-yeomanry cross country race in 1964, is seen carrying 76-mm Saladin rounds, 'bombing up' before the pinnacle of the training year: live firing the main armament.

Below: Rare images demonstrating the deep bronze green colour schemes of the armoured vehicles in the early 1960s.

Tpr Anthony Longdon joined the regiment in 1964, his first camp being Cranwich Camp near Thetford in 1965. In 1966, the RWY sent a composite squadron under the command of Maj. Alexander, who had previously served as a regular officer with the 7th Queen's Own Hussars, to Germany. Attached to the 10th Hussars on Luneberg Heath during World Cup week, Tpr Longdon was awarded best gunner in a competition against regular cavalrymen, thanks he told the author to a brilliant vehicle commander, Sgt Pete Speedy. Longdon is now a vicar in Wiltshire.

This visit to Germany was the first time the RWY had been integrated with a regular regiment. Following initial problems on the range, 'naturally things went wrong and Lt X had great difficulty in deciding the direction of the range let alone the target'; much valuable training was had there, and it was generally agreed this was an experience neither to be missed nor repeated. The yeomen, like generations of British soldiers before and afterwards, visited and enjoyed the distractions of the nightlife of Hamburg.

Warcop ranges in Cumbria, 1967. *Rear:* Unknown trooper, Cpl Dave Norman, and Sgt Pete Speedy. *Centre:* L/Cpl Frank Vennel, Sgt Geoff Webb, and Tpr Dolling. *Front:* Tpr Mick Salter and L/Cpl Trevor Wilkins. Anthony Longdon recalled a misfire with the main armament during this camp, which resulted in him having to carry the live shell down range to a safe distance.

The RWY Association open day in July 1971, which is still fondly remembered by retired yeomen and their families as Lord Margadale very generously allowed the use of his house and gardens. The photograph includes many veterans of the Second World War.

A Ferret armoured car crew at Salisbury Plain, 1973—a very different era from that of today's Army Reserve soldier. The title of the photograph was: 'The three musketeers, Athos, Porthos and Pushoff'—Bob Aland, Frank Vennell, and Terry Hart.

Above: Inspection of the Royal Yeomanry by HM Queen Elizabeth, the Queen Mother, at Tilshead, 8 May 1973. HM Queen Elizabeth, the Queen Mother, had graciously consented to become royal honorary colonel on the formation of the Royal Yeomanry Regiment, and this was her first visit to her regiment at annual camp. Accompanying Her Majesty is Col. the Hon. Gordon Palmer OBE TD DL, the honorary colonel of the Royal Yeomanry, and Maj. Peter Gregson MBE of 2RTR, the training major. A tactical display and an armoured car demonstration were followed by the inspection of Regimental Headquarters and the regimental echelon. The sabre squadrons then emerged, hitherto unseen, and dramatically advanced over the hillside in Ferrets and Saracens as regimental trumpeters, hidden in the woods sounded the advance and charge magnified across Salisbury Plain by microphones. Nine coloured rockets symbolising the nine constituent yeomanry regiments of the Royal Yeomanry were then fired from the hilltop.

Below: The mounted drive past in summer 1989 following the granting of the freedom of Trowbridge.

Above: A REME Foden 6 × 6 recovery vehicle recovering the top-heavy FV2721 Fox armoured car on the edge of Sidbury Hill on Salisbury Plain. Cpl Lyne REME with his back to the camera is directing the recovery operation.

Below: 'A' RWY Squadron annual camp, 1996. *Back row:* Sgt Turner, Cpl MacDonald, Cpl Blackwell, Cpl Mullen, Cpl Edwards, Cpl Comley, Tpr Cloughton, and Tpr Carson. *Third row:* Sgt Philpot, L/Cpl Lincoln, Bdr Cook, L/Cpl Ward, L/Cpl Griggs, L/Cpl Holmes, L/Cpl Williams, Cpl Powell, L/Cpl Gray, L/Cpl Wood, L/Cpl Aitken, Tpr Jackson, Tpr Ricks, L/Cpl Moore, Cpl Dobson, S/Sgt Chamberlain, L/Cpl McMartin, S/Sgt Griffiths, Tpr Burr, Cpl Williams, L/Cpl Cox, Sgt Court, S/Sgt Mullen, and Sgt Jones. *Second Row:* S/Sgt Pulford, S/Sgt Childs, Lt Mason, Capt. Guinness, WO2 Walters, Maj. Brooks-Ward, Maj. Hamilton-Russell, Lt Moss, Capt. Leighton, and SCpl Evans. *Front Row:* Tpr Osbourne, L/Cpl Osbourne, S/Sgt Cottrell, S/Sgt Stokes, Sgt Clinton, Tpr Taylor, L/Cpl Hart, Cpl Mason, L/Cpl Mead, Cpl Beel, and Tpr Crain. (*Image copyright Farrar/ Tempest Photography*)

Capt. Dominic Guinness went on to lead the squadron in Iraq in 2003 and later commanded the Royal Yeomanry; he is still serving in the Army Reserve. Maj. Simon Brooks-Ward was promoted to major-general as the most senior reserve officer in the British Army.

Above: HM Queen Elizabeth, the Queen Mother, visiting RHQ in Cavalry House, the Duke of York's Barracks in the King's Road in February 1997. S/Sgt Pulford, Cpl Holder, Cpl Comley, L/Cpl Mead, L/Cpl Farmer, L/Cpl Read, S/Sgt Chamberlin, and Tpr Read are standing to attention awaiting Her Majesty. Lt-Col. David Bone RDG and Maj. Simon Brooks-Ward are in attendance.

Left: 2Lt Conn MacEvilly in Iraq, 2003.

Above: A recruiting event in Trowbridge in the summer of 2003 following the squadron's return from Iraq—Capt. Ford, Tpr Horne, Cpl Williams, WO2 Pulford, Tpr Denman, and Tpr Hyde.

Right: Maj. (later Col.) Dominic Guinness MBE wearing RWY number one dress on the steps of Buckingham Palace.

HRH Princess Alexandra chatting to members of the squadron following the presentation of Iraq campaign medals—Cpl Burr, Sgt Blackwell, Cpl Williams, and Capt. Ford.

L/Cpl Mark Denman sitting right of picture and members of 'C' Squadron HCR near the end of the gruelling tour in Afghanistan.

Maj. Conn MacEvilly in RY 'blues' on parade with squadron officers carrying whips in 2012. Both the RY and RWxY had female officers badged to the RAC decades before the change in regulations concerning female soldiers in teeth arm units. Capt. Jules Ward pictured here was one such officer who went on to command a squadron in the RY. (*Image from Calyx Media*)

Brig. Simon-Brooks Ward presenting medals on a summer's evening in Swindon. (*Image from Calyx Media)*

Ewen Manor in July 1986. *Back row*: Tpr Tomley, Tpr Young, Sgt Chamberlin, Tpr Woodward, Tpr Lewi, and Tpr Giles. *Third Row*: Tpr Mercer, S/Sgt Cofferon, L/Cpl Smith. Sgt Lake, Tpr Miller, S/Sgt Sharpe, S/Sgt Guillou, L/Cpl Noble, Sgt Gumm, Sgt Webb, Sgt Atkinson, Cpl Quinn, Tpr Carson, Tpr Watson, Cpl Carter, Sgt Fry, Tpr Bailey, L/Cpl Dowdell, *Second row:* L/Cpl Peck, Cpl Fahey, Cpl Warren, S/Sgt Margetts, Sgt Quince, L/Cpl Coling, Cpl Mead, Sgt Springthorpe, Sgt Holbrow, SQMS Dinning, Sgt Littlefair, WO2 Wright, Tpr Greaves, Tpr Boyle, Tpr Thomas, Cpl Carrick, Tpr Norton, Cpl Long, S/Sgt Davis, and Cpl Griffiths. *Front row:* 2Lt Carpenter, Lt Field, Capt. Windsor Clive, Capt. Orme, WO2 Frankland, Maj. Arkell, Col. Morrison (Hon. Col.), Maj. Chamberlain, Capt. Lees, Capt. Mertens, Lt Gardner, Lt Raschen, and Lt Clutterbuck. (*Photograph copyright Borg photography*)

Ewen Manor in Gloucestershire was the home of the late Colonel Sir Martin Gibbs, who joined the RWY in 1937 and embarked for Palestine as a second lieutenant in 1940. He was mentioned in dispatches for operations on Yellow Ridge during the battle for Palmyra in Syria and awarded a DSO when commanding 'B' Squadron at El Alamein, where he was wounded in both legs. He was appointed 'Companion of the Bath' in 1958 and held the offices of high sheriff of Gloucestershire in 1958 and deputy lord-lieutenant of Wiltshire and lord-lieutenant of Gloucestershire. He was also honorary colonel of the RWY and the serving squadrons and old comrades were always warmly welcomed to Ewen.

Maj. (later Col.) Oliver J. H. Chamberlain QVRM TD FRICS. A long-serving Wiltshire Yeoman, Oliver joined 'A' (RWY) Squadron, the Royal Yeomanry in 1972 and was commissioned two years later. He transferred to 'B' Squadron, the Royal Wessex Yeomanry in 1976 and held a variety of regimental posts and commanded the regiment from 1990 to 1994. He was also the author's first CO.

He was SO1 1st Armoured Division, SO1 implementation team leader for the Dorset Yeomanry, Colonel Yeomanry, and his last appointment was deputy commander 43 (Wessex) Brigade. Oliver was awarded the QVRM in 2004 and has been honorary colonel to the RWY since that year.

The late Lt-Col. Bobby Faulkener from the 5th Royal Inniskilling Dragoon Guards leads the regiment on a march-past at annual camp. He was the first regular commanding officer and is commemorated by the 'Bobby Faulkener Prize' for the first faller at the Yeomanry Ride held at Badminton in November each year. Lt Guy Hankin, a keen polo player, is the tall RWY officer nearest the saluting dais.

The Series 3 Land Rover had many failings but was a simple vehicle, easy to conceal and maintain, and allowed more time to learn the craft of reconnaissance.

Sgt 'Paddy' Blair, right of picture, with the late Maj. Tim Clarke, centre picture, formerly of the Gloucestershire Regiment and HQ Squadron RWxY, discuss the day's rations on the Dorbaum Ranges outside Munster in September 1996. Blair served with the Royal Irish Rangers in Libya in the late 1960s and then for over two decades with 'B' and HQ Squadron RWxY rising to the rank of WO2. His cooking was infamous; if a soldier irritated him, he was known to respond by producing an almost inedible, fiery curry, and he will never be forgotten for the addition of boiled sweets to the range stew.

The Royal Wessex Yeomanry officers in Redford Cavalry Barracks in Edinburgh, 1997, prior to deploying on Exercise Deep Gorge 2. This would be the last time the yeomanry exercised as a whole as the gradual drift towards individual reinforcements and armoured training took over as the next millennium dawned. (*Image copyright Borg photography*)

Lt-Col. Selby-Bennett giving orders in a barn on Exercise Flying Cast. Capt. Tim Verdon, a talented polo player, the intelligence officer, and also a Royal Wiltshire Yeoman, stands behind the CO.

From left to right: the RSM, an attached French cavalry officer, Maj. Max Rothwell ('D' Squadron) who later commended the regiment; Capt. Patrick Long; Maj. Ben Adams ('B' Squadron); Maj. Nick Kelly ('A' Squadron); and the fatigued-looking adjutant Capt. Dominic Alers-Hankey, a successful amateur jockey who won the Grand Military Gold Cup in 1994.

Note the wine bottles in the background sitting next to 'Gamebird', the officers' mess drinks cabinet converted from a wicker basket and reputedly an old mule pannier. A glass of wine or whisky was offered to all at a briefing, which was a serious occasion as evident by the intense concentration on the faces of the majors in the front row.

The amalgamation parade of the Royal Wessex Yeomanry and the Dorset Yeomanry, Stanley Barracks, Bovington Camp, September 1999.

Above: Acting SQMS Sergeant Lackmaker and Cpl Bambridge during annual camp, 2000. Both were long-serving and popular chefs. Adrian Bambridge had previously served in the Royal Navy and was promoted to sergeant in 'B' Squadron, proudly serving alongside his son. John Lackmaker served for twelve years in the Army Catering Corps and RLC; his sister, Tracy Lackmaker, later joined the squadron, having completed twenty-two years as a regular army chef. The squadron chefs laboured for many hours both day and night to feed the yeomen, both on exercise and in camp, often routinely starting work at 4 a.m.

Below: RWY Challenger 2 tank crew in the twenty-first century. Jeff Timmins, a barber from Salisbury, pictured to the right of the main armament, served on convoy escorts on the Iran–Iraq border in 2005 during Op Telic 5 attached to the Royal Dragoon Guards. He went on to serve in Iraq again with the King's Royal Hussars, this time on long-range desert patrols covering the same ground as his predecessors in the 1940s. He later served in Afghanistan and was mobilised to help with the Olympics and on Operation Pitch Pole dealing with regional flooding in the south-west of England. He was awarded two lord lieutenant's certificates and left the regiment in 2015 to spend more time with his family. He always took his hair clippers on operational tours, charging cigarettes and 'fizzy pop' for a good haircut.

Above: Capt. Tim Knight, Lt-Col. (later Col.) Patrick Long, and Maj. Richard Morgan at the Army Cresta competition in St Moritz. Tim Knight served in both 'A' and 'B' Squadron and wears the short-lived but colourful RWxY pullover that included the red of Devon, Dorset, and Wiltshire, the buff of Gloucestershire, and the silver of the Yeomanry. Patrick Long is wearing the colours of the RWY and Richard Morgan, an experienced and successful Cresta rider, his Army jumper. Both Tim Knight and Patrick Long are actively involved in the running of the RWY Benevolent Fund, which is in place to support all Wiltshire yeomen, their families, and those that have served with the regiment, when they find themselves in need. The above officers have served on five operational tours from the Balkans to Iraq and Afghanistan.

Below: Capt. Henry Kemp-Gee from 'B' Squadron crashes on Shuttlecock corner wearing the traditional racing attire of heavyweight tweed and RWY pullover with his regimental tie to ensure he is correctly dressed for lunch. Although an expensive pastime and officer heavy, a few young and enthusiastic soldiers have taken up the challenge of this unique and exhilarating alpine sport. (*Images courtesy of Crestaphotos*)

'B' Squadron marching onto the parade ground in Fort Hood Texas in 2008. (*Crown copyright*)

Sgt Scott Rowe from Salisbury in the turret of an M1 Abrams. He joined 'B' Squadron in 1995 and was still serving as SQMS aged fifty-three in 2019. (*Crown copyright*)

Above left: Cpl Jim Martin, whose grandfather, Sgt P. C. Fielding, and great uncle, Anthony Rose, both served with the RWY before and during the Second World War.

Above right: Cpl Michael Gibbons taking cover during a firefight with the enemy outside Nawa in Afghanistan in 2009 while attached to 1st Queen's Dragoon Guards. The patrols would joke that the quicker they entered into a contact, the less walking was required, and bets were taken on how many hundreds of metres they would travel before the first shot was fired.

Below: Those who can recall the *Commando* comics of the 1970s and '80s will remember the thread that runs through many of these tales of daring-do—that of a square-jawed and tough British sergeant-major who saves the day. Les Welsh (above left) is that man—a proud Scouser, he first enlisted in the Parachute Regiment; served for twelve years with Special Forces (UKSF), reaching the rank of sergeant-major; and then, having relocated to Wiltshire, joined 'B' Squadron, the Royal Wessex Yeomanry. As is necessary with many SNCOs, he dropped to the rank of sergeant to continue soldiering but regained his rank of WO2 and will be remembered as one of the most colourful, enthusiastic, and professional squadron sergeant-majors.

A builder by trade, he was renowned for constructing props to act as targets for the reconnaissance land rovers, including a scale model of a Scud missile. He completed five operational tours of Iraq and Afghanistan, experiencing some of the fiercest fighting of those campaigns. His operational reports describe 'a stalwart of the tactical battlefield', 'demonstrating calmness under fire', and 'a father figure and inspiration to younger soldiers'. As a sniper, he took great personal risk and his actions saved many lives.

The author, who has worked with many high-quality individuals over two decades, feels privileged to have known and worked with such a man. (*Photograph courtesy of Philip Hannaford and The Sun newspaper*)

Above: The 91st Royal Armoured Brigade, the Jordanian Armed Forces, April 2004. Centre of picture is Lt-Col. Ben Adams, a former Royal Hussar and adjutant at Swindon, 'B' Squadron leader and commanding officer of Bristol University Officer Training Corps, seconded as an instructor for the UK gifted fleet of Challenger 1 Main Battle Tanks in March 2004. Retired, he is now chairman of the RWY Benevolent Fund. He is pictured with Capt. G. J. Evans KRH and Capt. N. Pennycock REME.

Left: RWY tweed. Very little is known about the heritage of this cloth, a bolt of which was discovered in the attic of Fonthill labelled 'RWY pattern tweed'. The red and yellow of the RWY colours are woven into the material, which possibly originated from the Isle of Islay, where Lord Margadale has an estate. Reviving this design as a regimental tweed was discussed at an officer's mess meeting in 2015, but sadly, sartorial taste has changed, and this smart garment owned by Maj. John Morgan may be the last of its kind.

Above: Lt-Col. David Utting in his role as the head of engagement for London District, escorting a group representing the Sikh community during a royal visit by HRH the Prince of Wales to Leicester.

Utting typifies many successful officers who have completed long careers alongside their civilian employment. He was commissioned into the Royal Navy in 1983, serving mainly in mine warfare and fishery protection. During this time, he also deployed on the ARMILLA Patrol during the Iran–Iraq war. In 1991, he joined 'B' Squadron, the Royal Wessex Yeomanry and over the next few years served in a number of posts at regimental duty; he took command of the squadron in 1999.

In 2002, he was selected for promotion to lieutenant-colonel and appointed to the Joint Services Command and Staff College as an instructor. He later commanded Birmingham UOTC and served in both Iraq and Afghanistan. (*Image Crown copyright*)

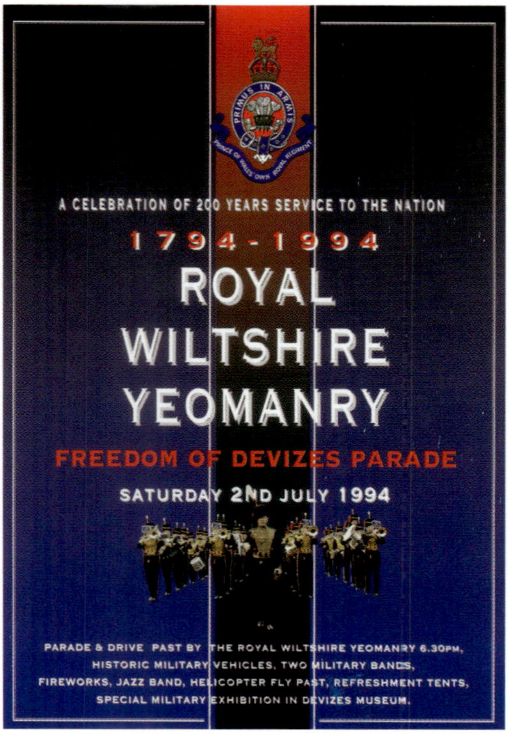

Right: The poster advertising the bicentenary parade in Devizes in 1994.

The impressive mounted escort at Devizes in 1994 displaying uniforms from the Victorian era to the First World War.

A march-past of the old comrades led by Col. John Peel brought to a conclusion this memorable parade, which was captured beautifully by the well-known military artist Joan Wanklyn.

Right: The Wiltshire Yeoman public house, a handsome former farmhouse dating back to the 1600s, now surrounded by a modern housing estate in Chilmark Road, Trowbridge. Royal Wiltshire Yeomen throughout the ages have had a passion for fine ale and cigarettes—the latter less so in modern times, but as recently as the 1990s, commanding officers 'orders groups' in the field were conducted in a haze of tobacco smoke in a twelve by twelve green canvas tent. There has always been a strong link with two of the great brewing families of Wiltshire—the Arkells in Swindon and the Bartholomews of Wadworth—in the regiment's spiritual home of Devizes.

Below: Col. James Arkell TD; unidentified RWY trooper; Sgt Andrew Pulford; Tpr Jason Hawkins, 'A' (RGH) Squadron Royal Wessex Yeomanry; and Maj. (Ret'd) Rupert Arkell TD outside Arkell's Brewery.

The new regimental flag is raised at Bovington Camp with the officers' mess in the background. It sits alongside the flag of 3 Armoured Division as the Royal Wessex Yeomanry finally unites to comprise Britain's fourth heavy armoured regiment. The new cap badge was not the end of the rebranding as a long and protracted change in all forms of dress was discussed; the regimental council finally settled for the new corporate colours of blue and buff. (*Crown copyright*)

Lt-Col. (now Col.) Christopher Macgregor with HRH the Earl of Wessex, wearing his RWY stable belt inspecting Ramrod Darcy III, the regimental mascot. (Crown copyright)

6

El Alamein: The Finest Hour

Lt-Gen. Montgomery inspected 9th Armoured Brigade on 30 September 1942, and as October dawned, the regiment kept busy with maintenance and practice demonstrations in preparation for what was to be the greatest battle of the desert war.

On 23 October, at 7 p.m., the RWY was formed up 3 miles short of the start line with the objective being Miteirya Ridge. Initial progress through the enemy minefields behind the New Zealand engineers was painfully slow, but before dawn, the tanks of 'A' and 'C' Squadrons exited this formidable obstacle; 'B' Squadron had now been reduced to only two tanks as the remainder had become casualties of undetected and torn-up mines.

Lieutenant Bartholomew's unpublished diary describes him wearing a smart new pair of cavalry twill trousers, sitting on his turret to gain better visibility as his tank passed through the minefield. There was a tremendous explosion as his tank hit a mine and subsequently threw a track but what was of greater concern to this young officer was the rip from top to bottom in his new trousers. Later during heavy fighting on the ridge, his tank was disabled and caught fire running down a German 88-mm anti-tank gun from the rear. The crew bailed out and started out towards the British lines but were captured. He continued:

> I should add that both my six pounder and Browning machine gun had jammed; my only weapon being my revolver which I used constantly from the top of my tank; with what success I am not sure.

Corporal Bill Rendell, who had joined the regiment in 1938, was a radio operator in Major Hubert Blount's tank, which was soon disabled; his diary records:

> It wasn't long before we were hit. The shot came in and touched my arm and went straight into the engine. We knew we had to get out pretty quickly as there were

> flames all around us. The squadron leader jumped out and he was badly burnt. The gunner was also injured and was blocking my escape route. I managed to push him out and we both fell off the tank.

Despite being under heavy fire, he managed to make his way to medical support and was treated by a captured *Afrika Korps* doctor and again cheated death as the jeep allocated to evacuate him hit a mine, badly wounding the other stretcher case. He was finally taken to a casualty clearing station where he learned that Major Blount, the bow gunner, and gunner were alive, but the driver (Lance Corporal Francis) had been killed.

The commanding officer had also been injured by a shell splinter during the battle and as the second in command was at brigade headquarters, Viscount Weymouth briefly took over until Major Gibb returned. Repulsing a counterattack of forty enemy tanks for the remainder of the day, the regiment took up hull-down positions on the ridge and continued to engage the enemy after replenishing with ammunition.

At 6 p.m., Major Gibb ordered the few remaining tanks of the regiment to retire to the brigade replenishment area where they rested, taking over and repairing replacement armoured vehicles. These were found to be in a shocking state four days before the second phase of the Alamein battle. The objective of the Miteirya Ridge had been taken, but what lay ahead was a far more daunting task, which would be recalled in years to come as the RWY's finest hour.

The second phase of the battle began on 1 November when the regiment moved in single file from its concentration area at El Alamein railway station. The visibility was appalling from a combination of darkness and dust from the vehicles. At 1.45 a.m. on the 2nd, following a ferocious and prolonged artillery barrage, the regiment again slowly advanced through their designated lanes in the minefields.

The enemy lay ahead across a saucer-like depression with the eventual final objective being a diagonal, ill-defined desert landmark known as the Rahman Track. Shortly before dawn on the 2nd, it became clear that the task ahead was monumental, the squadrons facing large numbers of well-concealed and powerful anti-tank guns. More importantly, the lead squadrons were now silhouetted against the dawn light; 'A' and 'C' Squadrons halted to engage on the flanks and 'B' Squadron advanced into what felt like the Battle of Balaclava, the cavalry charging guns head on with predictable consequences.

The RWY was eventually withdrawn from the line at 4 p.m. that day with only four tanks remaining. On 5 November 1942, the commanding officer, Lt-Col. Gibb, sat down and wrote a personal message to all ranks, ending with 'This action will be recorded in the annals of regimental history, and the epic of B Squadron will live for all time'.

In a letter home to his wife, Hubert Blount, commanding 'A' Squadron, described his part in the battle:

The late Reverend Adrian Heath, who served in the regiment during the 1950s, described to the author his childhood with 'the sounds of the RWY WW2 history ringing in his ears'. His father Ted, known as 'Heathy', was posted away from tanks a week before Alamein as Montgomery only wanted young men in armour and his father at thirty-three years old was one of the oldest men in 'C' Squadron. On the night of Operation Supercharge, he was driving the water bowser for 'A' Echelon through the first minefield and his vehicle was blown onto its side by German shellfire, trapping his father by the foot brake that had bent as the lorry rolled. A private soldier from the Gordon Highlanders climbed into the cab and removed his boot, then helped him out of the vehicle. After the war, these memories stayed with Ted, who would often wake up at night with a shout as he relived his experiences.

The Heath family have strong links with the RWY as Ted's brother Jack was a 'C' Squadron man, who became a dispatch rider for the HQ orderly room working for the RSM Jack Pike. He survived the war despite being blown off his motorcycle on numerous occasions.

We all, right down to junior NCOs knew exactly what we are fighting for and what we were up against and the plan and the intention not only of our little party but what was to happen along the line as well.

At about 9.30 p.m. our artillery barrage opened up with a crash and continued to fire rapid without a break until about 4.30 in the morning. It was supposed to be the heaviest concentration that has been produced in this war and it was certainly the most violent and spectacular performance and most inspiring, and either such a complete surprise or had such a shattering effect that practically nothing came back the other way!

We hung about for a long time, Henry, Chris and I leaning our backs against the warm parts of the Colonel's tank gossiping while we waited for the order to go forward. It was jolly cold and too noisy for normal conversation but company was welcome at that stage. Then the report came that the lane was cleared through the first minefield and we walked back to our tanks and started off.

I went in front because I had the squadron of big new Shermans which were the surprise packet, followed by Charles' squadron (C Squadron) which was to support me on my left with his Grants and then Henry (B Squadron) with his light chaps to be ready for a fast pursuit in case the Boshe [*sic.*] should run too fast for us slow old buffers.

There was a good moon during the early part and in the leading tank it was quite easy to see the markings of the lane and we got on very well 'til almost the end of the last enemy minefield by which time our own guns had lifted and the Hun had recovered from the first shock and we have a number of hold ups with dawn getting unpleasantly near. However, we got it cleared with about 20 minutes of darkness to go and I hurried up to the top of the ridge keeping my chaps at visibility distance behind me until I could see what was over on the other side. By the most extraordinary luck I and my next five tanks got through the mines and things on top of the ridge but all the rest of my squadron got into trouble. And exactly the same thing happened to Charles. It was almost a miracle, because after it got light no other tanks were able to get through all day, and the ones that were blown up on top of the hill drew all the enemy A/T gun fire giving Charles and I time to go forward and take up suitable positions according to plan. We had a most interesting and effective shoot against masses of disorganised guns and transport and every sort of stuff for about half-an-hour and then the panzer counter attack came in and we really got down to business.

We set the first line of six on fire when they were about 1500 yards from us and we could almost see the ones behind losing courage! Then I got hit from behind from one of the 88mm which had got left back on the crest of the ridge and I was not able to take any further part.

We did stop them as you know and the really classic battle was fought later of which the climax was Timmy's wonderful show with D Squadron [author's note: this is what was in the letter, presumably as a security measure]. Multiply our telephone number by five will give you our total casualties, far the greatest number only slightly wounded—we think ourselves awfully lucky.

An extract from Major Gibbs' Military Cross citation illustrates the experience of a squadron officer in the battle:

Throughout the action Major Gibbs led his Squadron with extreme courage and ability until his wireless set was shot from behind his head. His driver had his compass shot between his legs, but continued and overran enemy positions and it is estimated that his own tank destroyed four anti-tank gun positions and besides a significant number of German infantry. His tank was finally put out of action and he received a severe injury to his foot. In assisting one of the crew out of his tank he was again hit in his leg and was finally evacuated but not before he had endeavoured to rally his Squadron on another tank.

This officer throughout showed brilliant leadership and by complete disregard for his own safety showed a fine example to others. The success of the whole operation was largely due to him.

The most exciting time I had was that day when our tank was blown up when we broke the line at Alamein. We moved up through the minefields at nine o'clock at night, the CO came along and wished us all the best of luck. There was a bit flying about as we went through the gap and we spread out and went at the Jerry like the flames of hell. Everything opened up on both sides, there was dust and smoke so thick that you could hardly see.

This was about daybreak then we had been moving all night, and were feeling a bit tired, we all had our greatcoats on as nights in the desert are raw.

Anyhow, we got closer and closer to the Jerry lines and the battle raged faster, stronger and fiercer. We reached his infantry and ran over their trenches; they put up their hands by the hundreds but we had no time for them, we went on for his tanks and artillery.

Tpr W. J. Antill (324490) embarked for Palestine in February 1940 and served with 'A' Squadron. His first-hand account of the battle of El Alamein was sent home as a letter in September 1943.

Tanks were knocked out and burning on each side of us and the crews were baling out right in amongst machine gun bullets as thick as hailstones, it was that or burning to death trapped in a blazing tank which is not a nice way to die.

We were now only 300 yards from his guns, we had been hit a couple or three times. I saw the sparks fly off the front of the tank as a couple of shells glanced off. Our wireless mast was blown off and the internal communication was broken down and we had to yell like mad at one another to hear our voices above the din, the roar of the engines, the chatter of the machine guns and the crash of the big guns.

The inside of the tank was full of smoke and fumes from the cordite and gun-powder, we were nearly choked and our faces were black with sweat, oil and smoke. I glanced at the wireless operator and all I could see were the whites of his eyes. He was hurling the shells into the breech and I was sending them into the Jerry as fast as they would go through the barrel. Then a tank next to us went up having been hit by a German 88mm gun, the biggest he has. A lucky shot from my gun blew that and the crew sky high, all within a second, the shells must have passed in mid-air.

Then we got it right in the front, we were on fire in a jiffy, flames were licking up around my face and singed my eyebrows off. The tank commander was already gone, the operator followed me but the two drivers were killed straight out, we could not see them and their compartment was like a white-hot furnace.

I looked around and dropped like a log as there were Jerrys all around us and although the ground was flat as a table top, they did not see us or had no time to bother about us as they were pulling out as fast as they could.

One hard neck *Eytie* [*sic.*] fired at me as I started running into the sun as we did not know where we were but we knew the sun would take us towards the sea and our lines. He could not shoot straight and after half a dozen shots, the trench was out of sight. We were not out of danger, the three of us got right in the way of a machine gun nest and the lead came by us swish, swish, swish. The tank commander stopped one right through his chest and out of his back. As he fell, my mate and I caught him and dragged him into a tank rut about a foot deep. Before I could get out a field dressing, he was dead and we lay by the side of him as we could not move as the machine gun was still having a go at us.

After a bit we made a dash expecting it to be the end; I died about twenty times that day. We then caught another burst, dropped flat in the open with no cover at all as the bullets whistled round are heads. One went through the seat of my mate's trousers and another hit an empty bully tin an inch from my head.

I thought we had had it but God was with us and I could see our infantry a hundred yards away. We got up and ran like greyhounds and jumped into their trench only to get shelled again like hell.

A man on my right had a piece shorn straight off his thigh, if he had not been there, I should have had it through the belly. We got out and I fell in with a couple of New Zealand chaps and slowly and slowly we got out of no-man's land into our own lines.

I got separated from my mate and after wandering around for a bit but after two miles I ran into Dick and his lorry and I was soon aboard and he gave me a packet of fags as I had lost a couple of hundred in the tank. I collected some new blankets and an overcoat, scrounged some grub and some tea and drank half a bottle of rum and dug a hole, fell into it and went to sleep.

I was frightened to death that day and how I hated all the dead Jerrys that I saw although I thought a good job you are dead. I could tell you plenty as all the boys could, but its best forgot. Well I reckon I have told you enough for now.

By the way I found my mate the next day and he was alright.

Yours,

Jack

Lieutenant John Bartholomew, who was by now a prisoner of war, was marched 2 miles to the rear and held in a large marquee that was targeted by British shells, wounding many Allied soldiers. He slipped away and hid in a blanket store but was recaptured the next day and threatened with execution by a 'very blond young Gestapo officer'.

From North Africa, he was flown low over the Mediterranean to Bari in Yugoslavia, described as a 'large and nasty camp where thirty desperate and starving Yugoslav prisoners died each day'. In March 1943, he was then moved to a camp in a monastery near Naples, which was described as 'very attractive with better living conditions and a good black market'. In August, he was moved by cattle trucks to Germany where he jumped onto a passing train only to be recaptured when it was occupied by an entire German regiment.

By April 1945, he was held with 85,000 prisoners in a camp in Mooseberg, 350 men to a hut, until liberated by the US Army. Repatriated in May, his war years finished by guarding prisoners of war in Devizes.

Above: An exhausted but elated tank crew after the battle.

Below: A hazy but important image taken of a resting tank crew after the battle. Their faces reveal overwhelming fatigue.

Above left: Cpl Kenneth Davis and his tank crew following the battle.

Above right: Tpr L. V. Simpkins, killed in action at El Alamein, was the driver of a 'C' Squadron tank commanded by Sgt Linfield that was hit, lost a track, and then hit a mine when reversing. The commander was wounded as was the gunner but the crew crawled back to the New Zealand lines where Tpr Ken Batt, the radio operator, was asked did he need a drink; a tin of peaches was offered, and as he drank the juice, he heard a thud and looking sideways saw Simpkins hit in the head.

Returning to the regiment's story, after El Alamein, what was left of the RWY was sent to Alexandria to rest and indeed enjoy everything that the fleshpots in the city had to offer. A move to Cairo and a camp at Mena at the very foot of the pyramids followed. Cairo had remained a peacetime city, and some of these battle-weary soldiers certainly found the transition to metropolitan life difficult following the horrors of recent weeks.

Christmas 1942 was spent in the desert under canvas, allowing morale and regimental cohesion to improve with the officers traditionally serving a fine lunch to the men. During the last few days of 1942, the regiment moved once again to Aleppo in Syria.

Capt. the Earl Cadogan receiving his MC ribbon from Gen. Sir Harold Alexander, the commander-in-chief of Middle East Command on 28 December 1942.

Cpl Davis and his crew of the Sherman named Rodbourne.

Above left: Tpr Norman Hanney and Regimental Sergeant-Major Pike one morning before breakfast on the way back from El Alamein.

Above right: There are very few surviving images of Grant tanks. Tpr (later Cpl) Jack Clayfield on the right was one of the desert veterans who continued to serve with 'C' Squadron after the war.

The 9th Armoured Brigade's role in Aleppo was now one of internal security duty, but the conditions were very different from the last visit to Syria, with a relentless freezing wind sweeping across the exposed plain from the Taurus Mountains. Reinforcements from 2nd Royal Gloucestershire Hussars, who had been disbanded following their terrible losses in the western desert, now arrived and were integrated into the RWY.

A mounted ceremonial parade of the 10th Armoured Division was arranged for March 1943. The adjutant, Captain Thursfield, issued detailed instructions; vehicles were cleaned and painted, all ranks were now wearing battledress with pistols as the regiment followed the 3rd (King's Own) Hussars past the saluting base outside the Baron Hotel in Aleppo. The slightly odd tradition of having lances for a non-lancer regiment continued as two sentries with lances stood each side of the saluting base, the tanks traversing their turrets through 90 degrees, and the gun barrels dipping 10 yards before the salute. The war diary records soldiers being ordered 'to sit to attention in their vehicles in a smart and soldier like manner'.

Intensive training continued thereafter, and in April 1943, the regiment moved east from Aleppo to Dibsi on the right bank of the River Euphrates in Syria for a month of brigade and divisional training.

Above: Tpr Anthony Rose at the wheel of the CO's M3 White scout car during the parade in Aleppo.

Right: Tpr Williams, left of picture, wearing newly issued battle dress.

Officers from 'G' Squadron 2nd Royal Gloucestershire Hussars, who were posted to the RWY in January 1943. *Left to right*: Lt David Gilliat, Lt Michael Jeffery, Capt. Teddy Milvain MC, Lt Frank Norbury, Lt Ernest Taylor, Capt. George Boyd, Lt Ian Walker, and Capt. George Wareham. Intensive training continued thereafter, and in April 1943, the regiment moved east from Aleppo to Dibsi on the right bank of the River Euphrates in Syria for a month of brigade and divisional training.

Test firing the Sherman's 76-mm main armament in Syria.

The difficult task of working on a stripped-down engine in the desert; right of picture is Anthony Rose from 'B' Squadron.

Aleppo football team in 1942.

ALMESBURY

'C' Squadron in Syria—1st Troop Chippenham, 2nd Troop Cricklade, 3rd Troop Malmesbury, and 4th Troop Swindon.

Opposite above: The happy crew of the now rather aged Sherman Malmesbury II, a 'C' Squadron troop leader's tank in Syria. Following a lull in photography during the fighting, the squadron cameramen got back to work. 'C' Squadron was prolific in its use of photography.

Opposite below: A rarely seen view of the CO's Sherman tank Trowbridge displaying the New Zealand white on black fern leaf insignia still worn with pride by Wiltshire yeomen of 'B' and 'Y' Squadrons, the Royal Wessex Yeomanry today.

Scenes from Syria in 1943. Note the variety of uniform and non-uniform worn in the group of eight attending 'Navigation School'.

By May 1943, the regiment was regenerating and command had passed to Lt-Col. Alastair Gibb as Lt-Col. Sykes was still unfit for front-line duty following the wounds he received at El Alamein. Full anti-malarial precautions were ordered as summer clothing was issued and the brigade started moving west towards the Mediterranean via the ancient city of Baalbek on the Lebanese border and finally to coastal Tripoli, north of Beirut in Palestine.

Sherman tanks were by now ubiquitous, the Crusaders having been handed over to the 7th Queen's Own Hussars and beach landings and night driving through the mountains of Lebanon were now the focus for training. This continued for the remainder of 1943, and although there was some frustration about not being involved in active fighting, there was a relaxed atmosphere in the Middle East as part of the 10th Indian Division, and the yeomen received great support from those at home in Wiltshire.

By 31 August, the regiment, now based from a camp in Binyamina in Palestine, was at full strength with fifty-two diesel-powered Shermans and twelve new Ford Scout cars. A new war establishment for armoured regiments was published resulting in twelve M3 Honey tanks forming a recce troop commanded by the newly promoted Captain Balding.

A 9th Armoured Brigade parade was held on 22 October requiring further hard work prior to the inspection by Lt-Gen. Anderson, commander of III Corps, before a move to a camp at El Beddaoui, north of Tripoli. There was now a new emphasis on beach landing and refining gunnery skills, including learning the principles of high-explosive airburst and attacking concrete pillboxes that continued throughout the year and into the spring of 1944.

Major Blount recalled an incident in Syria that amused the mess but horrified the two attached American officers who were supervising Sherman training. Despite the limitations with rations and bathing facilities, life in the officers' mess continued as it would have in a tented camp at home. Viscount Weymouth discussed a prank with one of the staff, who, following a 'donation', was happy to oblige. During dinner one evening, Lord Weymouth summoned the waiter and pronounced the soup disgusting and proceeded to slowly pour it over the head of the unflinching fellow who then quietly retreated apologising for the quality of the night's fare. The officers at the table continued to chat and most did not even look up other than to view the horrified expression on the American officers' faces.

The Pembroke Arms with 'The Lamb' from 'B' Squadron on the right. Maj. Herbert is third from the right in the back row; to his left is Capt. Christie-Miller; and to his left is Capt. the Marquess of Lansdowne with his hands on his hips.

Tprs Davis, Marks, and Williams. The title of the photograph was 'ruins amongst the ruins'—the Temple of Jupiter Baalbeck in Syria.

RSM R. E. J. Pike MBE was originally SQMS of 'A' Squadron and the RSM from 1942 to 1945.

An extremely rare photograph taken inside a Sherman with Cpl Tom Cook, who transferred from 2nd Royal Gloucestershire Hussars with whom he was wounded at the battle of Knightsbridge in May 1942.

The officers in Syria, November 1943. *Rear row:* Lt J. P. S. Vowles, Lt A. E. Taylor, Lt A. O. Wheeler, Lt F. S. Rogers, Lt W .M. S. Jeffery, Lt D. F. Gilliat, Lt R. H. E. Brogden, Lt H. A. D. Wade, and Lt C. M. Austin. *Second row:* Rev. W. B. Haynes, Lt S. J. Elliott, Lt L. C. Wheeler (QM,) Capt. the Marquess of Lansdowne, Capt. G. G. Boyd, Capt. W. L. R. Balding, Capt. B. Holiday, Capt. R. S. Walker, Capt. M. V. O. Jackson, Lt P. T. Lawson, Lt G. S. Wills, Lt A. B. Clark, Lt S. S. James, Lt H. G. Wareham, and Capt. R. W. Davidson (RMO). *Seated:* Capt. M. W. H. Bell, Capt.F. A. G. Blackwood, Maj. The Earl Cadogan MC, Maj. C. E. Awdry, Maj. H. B. Blount MC, Lt-Col. A. M. Gibb, Capt. G. R. Thursfield (Adjutant), Maj. The Hon. A. E. G. Herbert, Maj. H. G. Awdry, Capt. S. V. Christie-Miller, and Capt. E. H. Milvain MC. *Seated on ground:* Lt J. Bilton, Lt P. Brittlebank, Lt F. Buckle, Lt A. B. W. Pennell MC, Lt J. Roberts, Lt G. M. Scott, Lt W. G. R. H. Leech, and Lt D. W. P. Bluett.

The crossed cavalry lances that were always placed outside Regimental Headquarters.

The RWY Contribution to the Long Range Desert Group (LRDG)

Periods of inactivity early in the Middle Eastern campaign had led to a handful of soldiers and officers leaving regimental duty in search of excitement; the Commandos, the Parachute Regiment, and the newly formed LRDG attracted a few such volunteers, and the RWY war diary records three such individuals leaving on 3 January 1941.

The Yeomanry patrol was added to the establishment of the LRDG in March 1941, the patrol being the basic formed unit of the group. Captain E. Spicer, a pre-war officer, took command of 'Y' Patrol (Y1) in late September–early October 1942 after the legendary David Lloyd-Owen had been severely injured during the Luftwaffe attack on the LRDG base at Kufra in Libya. Spicer subsequently led the patrol on operations until being transferred to Y2 in late January 1943. According to the LRDG war diary, he appears to have seen out the desert campaign with Y2, leaving the LRDG in May 1943 accompanied by his batman, Trooper 'Tich' Tanner, who served from September 1942 to 1945. Spicer's patrol carried out long-range reconnaissance for the Eighth Army watching the Tripoli road for a seven-day road census as his old regiment was engaged at El Alamein.

Trooper (Trumpeter) Anthony 'Tich' Cave MM 555726 ('B' Squadron RWY) from Rode Common in Somerset is one of the most remarkable of these volunteers. He served as a machine gunner with the LRDG from January 1941 until the end of the war refusing 'Python Leave' (his entitlement to return home after four and a half years' service overseas) in order to stay with the unit. He was captured with 1,500 Allied servicemen at Mechili in Libya on 7 April 1941 but escaped by walking over 200 miles through the inhospitable North African landscape and was promoted to lance corporal by October 1942.

Other confirmed RWY members of the LRDG included trooper Josiah 'Joe' McPike, originally a regular reservist cavalryman who joined 'A' Squadron RWY, serving on a Bofors truck (which provided heavier firepower with its 37-mm gun) with the LRDG from January 1941 until the end of the desert campaign.

Trooper Alf Withers from Hampshire was another ex-regular reservist from the 13th/18th Royal Hussars (QMO), who served with 'A' Squadron RWY, transferring to the LRDG in January 1941, and serving until September 1944.

Above left: A photograph of an LRDG group taken by David Lloyd-Owen, which dates the image before the arrival of Capt. Spicer. Tich Cave MM is shown in the upper left picture looking over the shoulders of two other patrol members.

Above right: Y1 Patrol Homs in Libya late 1942. Alf Withers RWY is extreme right back row.

Below: 'Y' Patrol in Homs, north-west Libya; Tich Cave is shown on the left in the front row.

Right: Tich Cave kneeling in front of the truck with his mate 'Mickey' Coombs of the North Somerset Yeomanry and Capt. David Lloyd-Owen.

Below: Above centre Tpr Richard 'Jigger' Lee, 'Y' Patrol, Giarabub in Libya 1941. He was an ex-regular reservist who served with 'A' Squadron RWY, leaving England for Palestine in 1940. (*Images courtesy of the late Harry Chard, Josiah McPike and Brian Springford from Y Patrol*)

7

The Italian Campaign

The 9th Armoured Brigade was now earmarked for the invasion of Italy, and on 24 February 1944, the regiment received the warning order to move to Egypt *en route* to Europe. The medical officer would have no doubt sighed deeply as he read the movement order, which insisted that 'all ranks and their baggage and equipment be inspected to ensure freedom from lice prior to embarkation'.

The RWY finally left the Middle East after four years of continuous service on 29 April, arriving in Taranto Bay in southern Italy on 4 May 1944. A move of 140 miles north by rail to Foggia followed where the Wiltshire yeomen, normally accustomed to real ale, began to get to grips with the rough local wine.

The squadrons were now split, supporting infantry battalions in countryside that was unfamiliar and hostile to armour—'A' Squadron supporting the 5 Buffs (Royal East Kent Regiment); 'B' Squadron, 6 Queen's Own Royal West Kent Regiment; and 'C' Squadron, the 8 Argyll and Sutherland Highlanders, all part of the battle-hardened 78th Division commanded by a capable cavalryman, Major-General Charles Keightley.

The objective was Rome, but this was not the open tank country of North Africa, with mountains on the right flank and rough, tight, and impenetrable olive groves and ditches everywhere. Throughout May 1944, the advance north continued slowly, and by 1 June, composite squadrons had to be formed due to the high attrition rate on the vehicles. Major the Earl Cadogan commanded one and Major Christie-Miller the other, both of which were engaged in heavy fighting.

Following this intense activity, a period of rest and regrouping was required as men were exhausted and vehicles severely tested. While at Alatri, 30 miles south-east of Rome, the commanding officer, Lt-Col. Gibb, relinquished command and was replaced by Lt-Col. Sam Lloyd, who had been serving as 2IC of the 3rd (King's Own) Hussars; he would remain in place until the end of the war. The war diary records the special order of the day from the outgoing commanding officer:

> On June the fourth, 1794, one hundred and fifty years ago, the Regiment was formed at Devizes. It is fitting that an anniversary such as this should come at a time when the name and reputation of the Regiment has never stood higher. You have fought these last five days a hard and difficult action, the results of which have been outstanding. You have been the spearhead of the Eighth Army attack, and I have been congratulated on the magnificent performance you have put up. It is a sad day for me as I am leaving you. We have had many good scraps together, and I look forward to the day, which I hope is not far distant, when we shall have a reunion in England. I thank you for the help and support which you have never failed to give, and I wish you, until we meet again, the best of luck and a speedy return to your homes.

The advance continued during June, north through Tuscany towards the River Tiber and the Gothic Line, a German defensive position in the Appennine mountains. Although the enemy was retreating, the fierce fighting continued through the towns of Citta della Pieve and Castiglione del Lago, south-east of Florence. The country was again close, and the gunnery training in Palestine was tested as high-explosive shells were frequently used against buildings.

'Under any skies'. The title refers to the privately published memoir consisting of the letters home from Lt David Gilliat from Brancaster in North Norfolk. He was commissioned generically into the Royal Armoured Corps and served with 2nd Royal Gloucestershire Hussars in North Africa, subsequently transferring to the RWY. His letters home describe the sometimes difficult transition from one yeomanry regiment to another. He was a popular and brave officer and was killed near Anghiari in Italy on 1 August 1944 when a mountain road collapsed and his tank rolled down a ravine.

On 15 July, 'B' Squadron had now left the regiment, and led by Major S. V. Christie-Miller, they fought through to Arrezzo attached to the 7th Infantry Brigade. Mines were an ever-present danger, and progress (like everywhere else in this campaign) was painfully slow. On 20 July, the ammunition expenditure was enormous, with tanks firing 430 high-explosive rounds and 25,000 rounds from the Browning machine guns.

A week later, 'B' Squadron (who were now attached to the Warwickshire Yeomanry) was supporting an attack on Badia San Veriano in Tuscany. Today, the hillside is overgrown, but in 1944, it was naked and exposed and half a mile ahead of Corporal Lawrence's tank; a leading Sherman hit a landmine and fell into the small churchyard below the road. The mountain road subsequently collapsed and the Shermans named *The Lamb and Upavon* fell 100 feet into a ravine, but remarkably, both crews survived. In 2017, Corporal Lawrence's son and grandson visited this site where they discovered remains of these tanks.

Throughout August, further heavy fighting took place, hampered by rain and poor road conditions; on the 20th, the much-respected Captain the Marquess of Lansdowne was killed in action when attacking Montedoglio north of Arezzo. There are conflicting accounts of his death, which include being hit by shrapnel and machine gunned. Only two weeks prior to his death, he had written to the parents of his friend, David Gilliat. This was to be the regiment's last significant action of the war.

Tpr Ken Batt, the radio operator, second from left in front of his Sherman 'Calne' in Italy 1944. This was the uniform that Ken described as 'rags', which he was still wearing complete with his issued Colt 38 revolver when he left Naples, homeward bound for Liverpool in 1944.

An unidentified Sherman crew in Italy.

A disabled *Panzerkampfwagen* Ausf A Panther, 1944 with unidentified officer and crew member, Tpr Cooling, and Cpl Lakey, who was killed shortly after this photograph was taken.

On 25 August 1944, the RWY's role in active war fighting came to an end when orders were received from Corps Headquarters that men with four and a half years' service overseas were to be withdrawn from active operations. This order now rendered the regiment ineffective as a fighting force as only three half squadrons could be put into the field. A period of rest near Lake Trasimeno in Umbria was granted with excursions into Rome and the disposal of equipment and vehicles.

These 'Python' personnel left for home on 12 October on the monarch of Bermuda, sailing from Naples. The Middle Eastern and Italian campaign was over, but the split had left fifteen officers and 336 men in Italy who were then posted elsewhere; three of the officers—Walker, Scott, and Awdrey—transferred to the 10th Royal Hussars (Prince of Wales' Own).

After ten days at sea, the RWY disembarked at Liverpool and travelled by train to Livermere Camp, north of Bury St Edmunds in Suffolk, where a regimental parade was held; here, the honorary colonel, Ulric Thynne (who had commanded before the war), Lt-Cols Sykes and Gibb, and Adjutant Captain Thursfield finally welcomed them home.

A month of leave was granted to all ranks before work started in December, converting crewmen to the Churchill tank. An important day that has had implications ever since was 2 December, when the message from Lt-Gen. Freyberg VC suggested the Fern Leaf as a new regimental insignia; it is still worn seventy-five years later.

Members of the regiment arrive at Trowbridge railway station on their return from Italy in 1944. For many, this had been a very long four years away from their families.

My Dear Lloyd

Your charming letter of 30th September, written on the eve of your departure from Italy has been left unanswered for a long time; not just because we were in any doubts but because I have been away from the Division after being injured in an aeroplane smash.

Yesterday I sent you and the Warwickshire Yeomanry a message answering your question.

Needless to say, we will be very proud to know you are continuing to wear the fern leaf as a reminder of Alamein days together. We have served with many formations and units during this war. No association was happier than that between the officers and men of the 9th Armoured Brigade and ours in the difficult days at Miteiriya Ridge and in the battle to break out. Those of us who saw your magnificent attack at dawn on the morning of the 2nd November will never forget it. Your gallant advance that morning, though at great cost, broke the gun line and was the turning point in one of the most decisive battles of the war. We are all very proud of the 'honorary New Zealanders' of the 9th Armoured Brigade who were members of the 2nd New Zealand Division, and on behalf of all ranks I send the Royal Wiltshire Yeomanry our best wishes.

With every good wish to you all for the future.

Yours sincerely

BC FREYBERG.

27th November, 1944.

In February 1945, the regiment started its new role in Suffolk, training reinforcements for Royal Armoured Corps regiments, the current role of the Royal Wessex Yeomanry seventy years later.

A gunnery wing, a collective training wing, and a driving and maintenance (D and M) wing were established, and in March 1945, the training of reinforcements on the Churchill tank began in earnest.

The 1st Royal Gloucestershire Hussars, the training regiment that had remained in the UK throughout the war, then handed over all training on the Sherman, Cromwell, and more modern Comet tanks to the RWY. The world was changing, as was the perceived threat, and the yeomen received lectures on democratic opinion, Russia and Poland, and Soviet foreign policy—signs perhaps of the impending Cold War.

As 1945 came to an end, the pace of life had become much slower as the regiment became a holding unit for those about to be released from service, and by early 1946, the RWY was placed in suspended animation.

A rarely seen but well-documented silver salver presented to Salisbury City Council by the regiment on their return to Wiltshire for a civic reception on 19 December 1945 prior to a cold and white Christmas.

Above: Gallantry awards were presented by HM the King at Buckingham Palace.

Below: The regiment in Livermere Camp, north of Bury St Edmunds in Suffolk.

8

Yeomanry Tales

The personal story of the RWY who fought in the Second World War is what makes any regimental history more readable and adds a degree of reality to the description of routine squadron and regimental movement and conflict. The following pages really illustrate the beating heart of the RWY.

Kenneth Batt, aged ninety-seven in 2018—one of the regiment's last survivor from El Alamein. Born in Swindon in 1921, Ken was a keen horseman before the war, and aged seventeen, he volunteered to serve with the St John Ambulance as he admitted he was feeling rather lonely. In 1938, his workmates at the Great Western Railway suggested joining the RWY to keep him busy. In a conversation with the author in December 2018, he recalled being interviewed by Sergeant-Major Allen, but at only seventeen, he was too young to enlist; like many, he attended days later claiming to be eighteen and successfully joined 'C' Squadron.

When war was declared, he was summoned to the office at work and told he was required at the drill hall in full marching order at 4 p.m. He slept at the drill hall that evening, where the troops were well fed with sandwiches and cakes by local volunteers. 'C' Squadron was moved by train to Wincanton where the weather was still mild, and contrary to the regimental history, which describes poor billeting arrangements, Ken found himself in the White Horse Hotel sleeping in the dance hall, his horse being 'C23' (Magregor). First parade was at 6 a.m. in the High Street and bathing facilities were available at the nearby Cow and Gate factory where the tanks normally used to make baby food became communal baths for cavalrymen. Ken's memories of later being billeted in a barn in Woodborough 7 miles north of Nottingham were the freezing temperatures and the German writing on the walls of the building that twenty years ago had housed prisoners of war. The MO, described by Ken as an 'old fashioned sort of doctor', ran his sick parade in the local pub.

Before the invasion of Italy, Ken and his crew started training for a raid on Crete, which never materialised, and later in the campaign, Ken recalled an RWY crew deploying to the beachhead at Anzio. When the crew later returned to the regiment, they were disappointed not to be granted the combined operations arm patch.

Capt. Hubert Blount MC TD DL was born at Ootacamund in India in April 1910. His mother died two weeks after his birth, leaving his father to bring the infant back to England. However, his father was to die himself four months later of wounds received at the Battle of the Marne. He was subsequently brought up by his grandmother and aunt, and after leaving Harrow, he was commissioned in 1930 into the 13th/18th Royal Hussars (Queen Mary's Own). The regiment had Lord Baden-Powell as honorary colonel and in 1931 had moved from Egypt to Sialkot in India. Here in India Blount enjoyed all the varied sports provided by regimental life, playing polo and cricket and made the most of his leave, hunting, shooting, and learning to fly, but at twenty-three, he left the regular army to marry and attend the Agricultural College in Cirencester. He subsequently bought a small farm near Tetbury and joined the RWY.

A pre-war image of Hubert Blount riding in the Beaufort Hunt point to point. In the early stages of El Alamein, having led the regiment through the minefields during the assault on Mitteirya Ridge his tank arrived on the forward slope at first light in support of the infantry. His vehicle was hit and set on fire but was not evacuated until the enemy counterattack had been repulsed. His MC citation read 'this officer throughout showed brilliant leadership and by complete disregard for his own safety showed a fine example to others. The success of the whole operation was largely due to him'. When one of his crew later visited him in hospital after the battle, Blount had to pick him up when he collapsed at the site of his squadron leader's burns. His son, Charlie, also joined the 13th/18th Hussars and then the Army Air Corps rising to full Colonel, and his grandson the musician James Blunt, the Life Guards.

Above: Hubert Blount in the turret of the George in Syria in 1943.

Left: Charles Edward (Ted) Bolton was born in Bexley Heath in Kent; his father was a keen follower of the turf and Ted was planning to start a riding school before the war, but when hostilities broke out in Europe, he was adamant he would enlist in a horsed cavalry regiment. He was one of the three RWY soldiers who settled in Bury St Edmunds after the war, having met his wife, a publican's daughter at the Three Kings pub in Fornham St Martin, north of Bury St Edmunds. He rarely spoke with his family of his time in the desert but religiously made the long journey back to Devizes for annual reunions.

Above: Ted Bolton undergoing basic training at the cavalry depot still wearing the General Service Corps cap badge before leaving the UK.

Right: Maj. Samuel Vandeleur Christie-Miller DL, CBE was born in 1911 and educated at Eton College and Christ Church, Oxford. He inherited the 4,500-acre Clarendon Park Estate near Salisbury on the death of his father in 1932 and served in the regiment throughout the war. He was a keen game shot all his life and a great countryman, holding many appointments in the county including high sheriff of Wiltshire in 1949–50 and deputy lieutenant from 1950. He was made CBE in 1965 for services to local government but died prematurely in 1968.

Above: Capt. Christie-Miller in the turret of 'Bolingbroke Arms' named after a pub near Wootton Bassett in Syria, 1943.

Left: Reginald Clifford holding oranges. He enlisted in the RWY in Wilton in 1932 and was promoted to corporal in 1939; he left the UK for Palestine with RHQ. In 1940, the first of his postings away from the regiment started when he was attached to the recently formed Pioneer Corps as a clerk in the depot at Sarafand, south of Haifa. Thereafter, he was promoted to sergeant and commissioned into the general list in 1942. In November 1943, he joined the Special Operations Executive (SOE) in Cairo and later served in the finance department as part of Force 133.

Right: Reginald Clifford.

Below: SOE staff in Bari, with Reginald Clifford right of picture. The unit controlled SOE operations in the Balkans based from Bari in southern Italy where he recalled issuing gold sovereigns as currency to agents in the field. Clifford returned to England in 1944 as part of the Python programme and was demobilised in 1946; he later re-joined the Royal Army Pay Corps in 1951, retiring as a captain in 1968.

Above left: Cpl Kenneth Albert Davies 557429 (1921–2000). Born in Swindon, he worked at the Garrard Engineering Works prior to the war; his father was a former Swindon Town footballer. Kenneth enlisted in the RWY at the age of fifteen, passionately fond of horses (there are inconsistencies in the recruiting documentation that confirm this). In peacetime, he would cycle 10 miles from Swindon to Cricklade on a Sunday morning to get the chance of a ride. In August 1939, aged only seventeen he was mobilised to the Middle East serving with 3 Troop 'C' Squadron. He was subsequently mentioned in dispatches at Mersah Matruh. Many of the 'C' Squadron photographs came from his personal collection donated by his family.

Above right: Tpr Bernie Blewett. On the sea journey from Marseille to Haifa, he recalled dumping the horses' manure overboard at night to avoid the tracking U-Boats. When on watch on deck with a junior NCO, a mine was spotted floating towards the ship and the NCO told him to shoot it with his rifle before it hit the boat. Luckily, a Royal naval officer saw them and sprinting towards the pair pulled the rifle away from Bernie because the mine was so close that any shock wave would have fractured the ship's hull.

He was at the siege of Tobruk and 'obtained' an Italian motorcycle, becoming the troop despatch rider purely because he wanted to ride a bike. He then went on to serve in Iraq and El Alamein, at one point serving as the marquess of Lansdowne's driver. His photographs were taken with a Box Brownie camera.

Herbert Daw was born to a farming family in Wotton-under-Edge, Gloucestershire in 1915. He was a gifted horseman and in 1938 enlisted in Malmesbury. When mobilised in 1939, he rode from village to village on his horse Acrobat, collecting fellow yeomen on the way. His mount travelled with him to Palestine, and like many troopers, he felt great guilt when upon mechanisation, his thoroughbred was sold to locals. He served throughout the Middle Eastern campaigns but was taken prisoner at El Alamein. At his funeral, Maj. Charles Bartholomew drew aside his son, Tim, and told him the story of how he was captured:

> The tank was hit and disabled and Herbert was able to escape unscathed but another crew member was trapped by his arm (Ted Domoney). Herbert returned to the damaged vehicle and amputated the injured man's arm at the elbow to free him and stayed with him to care for him until they were captured.

His son described to the author a unique and strange recollection that came back to him after being told this by his father's old troop leader:

> When we were little we were watching a war film where a tank crew were calmly leaving a stricken tank and uncharacteristically Herbert said to his children something about that wasn't how you got out of a burning tank and that he knew someone who had gladly had his arm cut off to escape.

Herbert always told his son that Lt John Bartholomew saved his fellow troops' lives when they were prisoners in Italy as he was able to use his rank to buy food for them. Herbert never forgave the Italians for their shocking treatment of prisoners of war but did relate how the prisoners would all whistle the theme to Laurel and Hardy as the Italians tried to perform a guard changing ceremony with comic results.

Scenes from the German POW Camp *Stalag* IVA near Dresden in Saxony.

A photograph taken in 1948 when Herbert was farm manager at Cirencester Park in Gloucestershire taken at Lord Henry Bathurst's twenty-first birthday party. Herbert, wearing white tie, is seen chatting with the 8th Earl, wearing 10th Hussar uniform, and took great pleasure in boasting that he rose to the rank of corporal in the war. Earl Bathurst's son, the Hon. Alexander Bathurst, served with the Royal Hussars (PWO) as a regular adjutant to the Royal Wessex Yeomanry and then as a long-serving yeoman with the author.

Charles Edward (Ted) Domoney (327629) was born in Wallsend, Newcastle-upon-Tyne, in 1918. On completion of his cavalry training at Redford Barracks in Edinburgh, 'Trooper Ted' was given leave and then ordered to report to the Fourth Cavalry Training Regiment at Colchester in March 1940.

He arrived in the Middle East in the autumn of 1940 expecting to join the Royal Scots Greys, but due to an administrative error, he joined the RWY. He deployed to Iraq and Syria and fought at Palmyra; his son recalls him describing the final assault when he and his mates armed with Thompson sub machine guns loaded with drum magazines had chased the Vichy French Foreign Legionnaires through the pillars at Palmyra. This intense dislike of the Vichy French appears to be commonplace amongst the yeomen.

He served as a wireless operator/loader in a troop leader's tank which was hit by an 88-mm German anti-tank gun at dawn during the attack on Miteirya Ridge. When his Sherman was hit, it caught fire and the commander who had been sitting on top of the turret was blown off. The gunner was killed while the driver, Tpr Daws, escaped from the tank and started to run for cover. Looking over his shoulder, he saw Ted hanging in the remains of the shattered turret and doubled back, carrying him to cover while the tank burned and its ammunition exploded. The remnants of the crew waited and soon a British jeep joined them. There was no room for all of the remainder of the crew, and only the tank commander was taken back in the jeep. The two remaining troopers waited to be rescued but were captured by a German patrol and taken to a German field hospital. Ted's left arm was so badly damaged it was amputated above the elbow.

Ted became a POW in *Stalag* IX A/H, a large monastery in Kloster-Haina South of Kassel in central Germany, which was chosen as a POW camp to house injured prisoners in the monks' cells. The repatriation process via the Swiss Red Cross started in the middle of 1943. He first landed in Sweden and then sailed to England by hospital ship in late 1943; he was then moved to a military hospital for examination. Ted finally met his mother and father at Newcastle-upon-Tyne railway station on 23 November 1943; while on leave with other local POWs, he was introduced to the lord mayor.

Ted's mother wearing an RWY sweetheart brooch. (*Photographs and this remarkable story from Ted's son Mick Domoney*)

Norman Hanney was born in Bradford-on-Avon and baptised at the Holy Trinity Church, an association that was to continue throughout his life. After leaving school, he started working for Wiltshire County Council; for him and some of his friends working at County Hall, one of the attractions of the RWY was the opportunity to ride.

Norman joined Headquarters Squadron in 1938 when some of the RWY's officers were councillors for whom he worked. After mobilisation on 3 September 1939, and a spell at Wincanton, he was billeted with HQ Squadron rather uncomfortably at Lowdham in Nottinghamshire.

He recalled the train journey south through France when at one station, a horse escaped into the ladies' waiting room with resulting shrieks of '*des chevaux, des chevaux*'. Norman fondly remembered his own horse, Jessica, as being very good-natured, but he recalled the challenge in the cavalry era of riding his horse and two others through a forest in Palestine, as he guided all of them the same way around each tree.

In the Syrian campaign, he and a mate had a lucky escape when straddled by bombs during the incessant air attacks from the Vichy French during the advance to take Palmyra. Eventually, after many days of bombing, Australian aircraft arrived and shot down some of the Vichy planes. At that point, Norman later wrote, 'we cheered like heck.' He sent numerous photographs and letters including some of Palmyra, Babylon, and Baghdad to his sweetheart Joan, whom he married in 1949.

At El Alamein, the Regimental HQ tanks were hit in the second tank charge on 2 November; Lt-Col. Gibb and others, including Norman, were able to get out just in time, but Sgt Pickford was killed almost immediately by machine gun fire. On his return to the UK in October 1944, he noticed that the beer in Bury St Edmunds, where they were camped, was weaker than when they had left England. In his demobilisation testimonial for Norman, Lt-Col. the Earl Cadogan referred to Norman's sobriety despite like all soldiers enjoying a pint of beer. The Bury St Edmunds experience left him with a life-long suspicion of Greene King.

After demobilisation Norman returned to his job at County Hall and always enjoyed the regimental reunions in October. He was always proud of the high esteem with which the RWY was held by the 2nd New Zealand Division; when visiting New Zealand in 2000, he was amazed to see that the copy of a portrait of Gen. Montgomery at the top of the staircase in a serviceman's club appeared to have no nose. It turned out that on their way into the club the veterans would rub his nose for luck, and over the years, it had vanished.

At the funeral of his Bradford-on-Avon comrade Denis Uncles, he met Colonel David Part, then chairman of the RWY Old Comrades Association, who persuaded Norman to take over as honorary secretary. They subsequently worked together until 2011, helping veterans of the regiment and their widows.

Norman died in 2013, just after his ninety-third birthday. Colonel Part gave one of the addresses at the memorial service to one of the last few survivors from El Alamein whose ashes were interred to the sound of the Last Post.

Bernard Fergusson, a distinguished officer of the Black Watch, in his short biography of Field Marshal Wavell refers to a highly secret document containing orders to verify various claims of acts of sabotage carried out behind the Vichy French lines in Syria involving Prince Aly Khan of the RWY. Very little has been written about this flamboyant and internationally famous member of the regiment shown above with Aitmadi Kassam Kothari while visiting the Ismaili community in India in 1942.

Born in 1911, Prince Aly Khan, the son of the Aga Khan, the leader of the Ismaili Muslims, joined the French Foreign Legion in 1939 and was posted directly to the then cosmopolitan city of Beirut. Disillusioned with the Vichy French in 1940, he joined the RWY; the war diary records him coming onto the strength in November of that year.

His biography records him encountering the RWY at a reception camp for the many French servicemen moving into British held Palestine at El Mansura but at this point the regiment was based four hours away on the coast at Hadera. What is certain is that the prince knew some of the aristocratic RWY officers prior to the war, including Lord Weymouth and the Earl Cadogan, who was married to his wife's sister.

Very little time was spent at regimental duty as word of his recruitment, knowledge of Syria and its people, and ability to speak multiple languages reached military intelligence in Cairo where he was rapidly posted, working alongside the eccentric Lt-Col. Alfred Wintle.

He went on to participate in the Allied landing in the south of France as a liaison officer with the US Army; for this, he was made an officer in the Legion of Honour in 1950 to complement his *Croix de Guerre* and United States Bronze Star. The prince ended the war as a respected Lt-Col. and in later life would say that his time spent as a soldier was some of his happiest.

TO THE BELOVED MEMORY

OF

CHARLES

7th MARQUESS OF LANSDOWNE

CAPTAIN, ROYAL WILTSHIRE YEOMANRY

and his brother

LORD EDWARD FITZMAURICE

LIEUT. IRISH GUARDS

KILLED IN ACTION, AUGUST, 1944

ST. MARY'S CHURCH,
CALNE.
July 14th, 1945.

The Most Honourable Charles Hope Petty-Fitzmaurice, seventh marquess of Lansdowne. Born in 1917, the second of the three sons of the sixth marquess, whom he succeeded in 1936, he was educated at Eton and at Balliol College, Oxford. In 1939, he was gazetted a second lieutenant in the RWY and went on active service overseas early in 1940; he was wounded in North Africa after taking part in the El Alamein action.

He was killed in action on 20 August 1944 at Monte Doglio in Italy. The mechanism of his fatal wounding is unclear and two possibilities are that his tank received a hit on the engine deck while his head was out of the turret, but Tpr Ken Batt told the author he had heard he was machine gunned. His crew bailed out and were taken prisoner. His younger brother, Lt Lord Edward Fitzmaurice, was also killed in action serving with the Irish Guards in France.

He was clearly a very popular troop officer. Many of the families interviewed by the author recall their fathers talking of him with great fondness. The oil painting from Bowood House above was painted posthumously by Sir Oswald Birley in 1946 and was kindly supplied by the current marquess, who served in the RWY in the 1960s.

M. H. J. Lawrence (324477) was born in Wiltshire; his father worked as a tenant farmer for Lord Bath. Like many, he enlisted underage with a group of friends in 1939 and surreptitiously was visited by his mother in Nottinghamshire on Christmas Eve 1939—the last time she would see her son as she died four months before he returned to England. He recalled the freezing temperatures on the long rail journey through France and having to break the ice on water buckets in the trucks shared with the troop horses.

In Palestine, while riding one but leading six horses, he fell and was dragged with his foot still in the stirrup which led to a limp in later life. He served throughout the Middle East with 'B' Squadron, including at Tobruk alongside his brother, Tom, who was the squadron clerk. As an instructor, he was deliberately held back prior to El Alamein, at which point he came close to death from malaria. Promoted to acting sergeant at the end of the war, the army wanted him to stay on but John returned to farming in Marridge Hill Ramsbury near Marlborough, eventually retiring to Market Lavington. (*Courtesy of Douglas and James Lawrence, son and grandson of John whose diaries were sadly partially destroyed at Orvieto in Italy in 1944*)

Robert Edwin Shipman was born in the Chelmsford district in 1922. He worked as a carpenter and was married in 1941 and had a son. Robert enlisted later that year and was posted to the Royal Armoured Corps and subsequently served as a trooper (7951524) in the RWY. In this photograph, he wears the generic RAC cap badge. Robert was killed in action at El Alamein on 2 November 1942 and today lies with others from his Regiment in the El Alamein War Cemetery in Egypt.

Capt. Lyndsay Thomas (Tommy) Murdoch was born in 1911 and gazetted a lieutenant in the RWY in November 1940. He volunteered for duty with Number 11 (Scottish) Commando, serving with 2 Troop, whose physically demanding training took place on the Isle of Arran.

This sub-unit was commanded by Capt. Geoffrey Keyes, who would later be awarded a posthumous Victoria Cross when leading the raid on Rommel's headquarters in November 1941. There is evidence that the relationship between Keyes and Murdoch, who appears to have acquired the name 'Stinker', was certainly strained during his time with 11 Commando, as was Keyes's relationship with other officers, including the legendary Paddy Mayne, who at one point was arrested for a dispute with his CO.

Murdoch was reported missing, presumed a prisoner, two days before Christmas in 1941. In July 1942, while a prisoner at Campo 35 in Padua in Italy, he joined members of the LRDG on construction of an escape tunnel that was finished in September of that year. The thirteen escapers dispersed into smaller groups and Murdoch accompanied Capt. Richard Carr MC, walking for seven days towards the Swiss frontier wearing battledress and clothes dyed with walnut stain to alter their appearance.

While in the Italian mountains, they both became soaked and were forced to find shelter in a local farm in Titopopenza; the farmer fed them but also handed them over to the Carabinieri police who put them in chains and were described by Carr in his report as 'thoroughly unpleasant'. A week was spent in the cells prior to a transfer to *Campo* 5 in Gavi where a further month was spent in solitary confinement; it had now become apparent that the Germans would soon be taking over and moving the prisoners back to Germany.

Murdoch and Carr teamed up once again for their second escape attempt, removing earth from beneath a staircase and laying down supplies of Red Cross food, following which the entrance to the foxhole was sealed with cement one hour prior to the proposed departure to Germany. The lack of air and cramped conditions soon became a problem, and a ventilation hole was drilled in the wooden stairs, allowing the escapees to access fresh air for fifteen minutes at a time.

The Caribinieri had now realised that the prisoners were missing and Italian Colonel Gusseppi Muscatelli described in Carr's report as a 'very bad type' suggested to the Germans that they break into the staircase. The prisoners, naked due to the stifling heat and starved of oxygen, were given another swift beating and moved by rail into Germany. Murdoch was eventually interned in *Oflag* IX A/Z in Rotenburg an der Fulda midway between Frankfurt and Hannover and would have taken part in the infamous forced march to the east where he was finally liberated. (*Image courtesy of the National Museum of Scotland*)

Sgt P. C. Fielding (above second from right) served in 'B' Squadron before the war, and although mobilised, he did not deploy overseas as he was a Wiltshire farmer. He was involved with procuring horses for the regiment and was deeply upset when many of them were destroyed on mechanisation. He later commanded the Worton and Marston Home Guard detachment south of Devizes.

Anthony Rose in Syria in April 1943; he served with HQ Squadron and his daughter married Sgt Fielding's son. Continuing the family tradition, Sgt Fielding's grandson, Jim Martin, proudly served as a corporal with 'B' Squadron during the author's service.

L/Cpl Charles (Lofty) Marston 558097 (1919–1997). Originally from Norfolk, Lofty was raised by his grandparents in Blandford in Dorset as his parents worked as travelling theatre players. He joined the RWY before the war and was mobilised with HQ Squadron in September 1939. While in Palestine, he was baptised in the Red Sea and accompanied the *padre* on an excursion to Jerusalem. He served throughout the war, and in later life, he was passionate and proud of his time with the regiment.

Lofty Marston shown right of picture in front of the tank Shearwater from the Longleat troop.

Len Oakley was born in Shropshire where his father was a stud groom. The family moved to Wiltshire where Len worked as whipper-in to the Avon Vale and Wylye Valley Hunts, enlisting in HQ Squadron in Trowbridge in April 1939.

Later in life, he recalled the sea journey to Haifa and the difficulty even an experienced horseman had of keeping two horses calm in rough weather. He served on operations throughout the Middle East other than for a few months when, as an expert horseman, he was attached to the Cavalry School in Palestine. He was clearly an exceptional equestrian as after the war, he was offered a number of positions with hunts throughout the country. Always a keen dancer, he met his future wife while stationed in Bury St Edmunds where he settled after the war, working as a chauffeur for the director a large, local engineering company.

He rarely spoke of his time with the regiment but maintained an interest in horses throughout his life and was a regular attendee at local point to points and Newmarket Racecourse and a keen follower of the local Suffolk Hunt. His memory of Italy was 'the chickens run in the front of the houses and out the back door, why would you want to visit?'

Tpr Denis Strachan was born in Enfield in 1919, but his family subsequently moved to Chippenham. At the outbreak of war, he was in a reserved occupation, working as a pattern maker for Westinghouse and he did not have to volunteer. His father had served with the City of London Imperial Volunteers in the Boer War and received the freedom of the city; this may have motivated Denis to enlist.

His pay book recorded an enlistment date of December 1938 at Chippenham; he chose the RWY as they were a cavalry regiment and he loved horses. He served in 'C' Squadron throughout the war with his mates Powell, Butler, Lovelle (known as 'Fingers'), and Banks and was a keen sportsman playing rugby and boxing.

A story that he passed down to his son recalled his troop moving in convoy, each tank having its own allocated position; on one occasion, his vehicle was not in its set place in the convoy and the tank that had taken Denis's position was hit and the crew killed. Following demobilisation, he returned to his previous occupation but moved to Lymington in the New Forest. Aged seventy-six, Denis moved to Perpignan in France and passed away just three minutes into his ninety-seventh birthday, having been married for almost sixty-six years. He always described his war as 'marvellous.'

Ken Sturmey from Swindon was lucky to leave Wincanton without a charge as he left his rifle behind when leaving the racecourse, but he subsequently embarked for Palestine in December 1939 and was one of the early volunteers for the SAS. He served with distinction with 1 SAS Regiment, parachuting into occupied France to fight with the maquis in the Morvan region. His family next saw him in 1943 following his wounding, which still lists him as a serving Royal Wiltshire yeoman. He married his childhood sweetheart Doris two days before Christmas 1944 in St Augustus Church in Rodbourne, Swindon. In 2018, the author interviewed his daughter who recalled he knew David Stirling and Paddy Mayne, the founders of the SAS; the regiment sent a large contingent to Ken's funeral. (*Images from the Rodbourne Historical Group*)

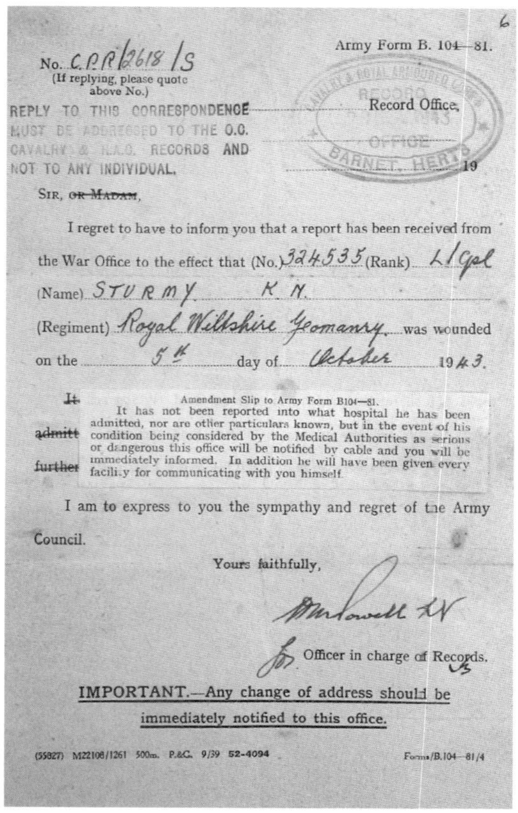

6

Army Form B. 104—81.

No. C.P.R/2618/S
(If replying, please quote above No.)

REPLY TO THIS CORRESPONDENCE MUST BE ADDRESSED TO THE O.C. CAVALRY & R.A.C. RECORDS AND NOT TO ANY INDIVIDUAL.

Record Office,

CAVALRY & ROYAL ARMOURED CORPS RECORD OFFICE BARNET, HERTS

19

Sir, ~~or Madam~~,

I regret to have to inform you that a report has been received from the War Office to the effect that (No.) 324535 (Rank) L/Cpl

(Name) STURMY K. N.

(Regiment) Royal Wiltshire Yeomanry was wounded on the 5th day of October 1943.

Amendment Slip to Army Form B104—81.

It has not been reported into what hospital he has been admitted, nor are other particulars known, but in the event of his condition being considered by the Medical Authorities as serious or dangerous this office will be notified by cable and you will be immediately informed. In addition he will have been given every facility for communicating with you himself.

I am to express to you the sympathy and regret of the Army Council.

Yours faithfully,

for Officer in charge of Records.

IMPORTANT.—Any change of address should be immediately notified to this office.

(55827) M22108/1261 500m. P.&C. 9/39 52-4094 Forms/B.104—81/4

Stanley Ronald Williams, 557461 (1920–2014), was born in Swindon and as a child had a love of horses, so much so that he would slip into the local Co-operative dairy yard just to see them. In later life, he would recall wandering through the horse lines in 1928 when the regiment was camped at Marlborough with not a care in the world aged only eight years old. Stanley enlisted in Swindon in 1939 primarily to gain access to horses and worked for a while as batman to the marquess of Lansdowne and clearly admired this officer as in later life, when talking of his death, he would become upset.

His passion for riding remained in later life, riding once or twice a week at the Talland Riding School near Cirencester, continuing with dressage and jumping until he was eighty-eight. After the war, he spent two years working in his old job at the Swindon Railway Works and then travelled the world with the Merchant Navy as a refrigeration engineer. Talking of the war brought mixed emotions, including great sadness, but his son felt he loved his time spent with the regiment. He was buried with an RWY flag on his coffin.

Swindon II 146777. 'C' Squadron troop leader's tank.

THE ROYAL WILTSHIRE YEOMANRY

Dear Sir,

The Royal Wiltshire Yeomanry, serving overseas, have their home county constantly in their thoughts and have named all their tanks after the various towns, villages, etc. in Wiltshire.

They have asked me to send you the enclosed photograph of the particular tank which bears the name of your Town and, hoping you may find it of interest,

I remain,

Yours sincerely,

[illegible] Colonel.

Honorary Colonel Royal Wiltshire Yeomanry

Left: Sgt Eric Woodman MM (1921–2009). Born in Kingston St Michael in Wiltshire, he attended the village school until aged fourteen and then trained as a butcher at the Co-op in Chippenham. He joined the RWY at the outbreak of war in 1939 and recalled sharing a railway truck with the troop horses on the long journey through France to Marseille. He initially served as a wireless operator and clearly recalled the squadron leader giving the order to charge at El Alamein; he was later awarded the military medal during the battle at Monteleone in Italy. He returned to England and met his wife Joyce at a Co-op dance when the regiment was at Livermere Camp in Suffolk, where he eventually settled. Eric had always been a keen sportsman, but above all else, he was devoted to his family.

(17115) Wt.41211/1452 50,000 2/41 A.& E.W.Ltd. Gp.698 Forms/W.3121/7. Army Form W. 3121.

9 Armd Brigade 78 Inf Division 13 Corps

Schedule No. .... (to be left blank) Unit ROYAL WILTSHIRE YEOMANRY - RAC

Army No. and Rank 324071 W/Cpl

Name ERIC WOODMAN (Christian names must be stated)

Date recommendation passed forward	Received	Passed
Brigade		
Division		
Corps		
Army		

Action for which commended (Date and place of action must be stated)	Recommended by	Honour or Reward	(To be left blank)
On June 16th this NCO was the crew commander of the leading tank of a half-squadron which was sent to mop up a pocket of enemy resistance one mile EAST of MONTELEONE, which was causing a threat to the flank of the main column. In closely wooded country Cpl. WOODMAN succeeded in spotting and knocking out an enemy anti-tank gun thereby causing the enemy to withdraw from an important part of their position. During this action his own tank was hit and four of the crew including himself were wounded. In spite of his own wounds, which were in the leg, and through intense shell and mortar fire, he succeeded in carrying two of his crew back to safety. Throughout this action, as in all the operations in which he has taken part, this NCO showed complete disregard for his own safety and his coolness and courage were an inspiration to all. (Signed) S. L. LLOYD. Lieut. Colonel. Commanding Royal Wiltshire Yeomanry.	S. L. LLOYD. Lt.Col.	MM	

9

The Post-war Era

In 1947, the Territorial Army was reformed with the regiment under command of Lt-Col. the Earl Cadogan. The following year, National Service was introduced, which included a compulsory period of time spent with the TA, a concept that was initially extremely unpopular with National Servicemen but eventually gained acceptance. RHQ was reopened in Bythesea Road in Trowbridge, housing a sabre squadron, with the remaining three sub-units based in Warminster and Salisbury, Devizes and Chippenham, and lastly Swindon. The squadrons were commanded by wartime officers and the familiar names of Herbert, Christie-Miller, Awdry, and Bartholomew allowed continuity into this new era.

The honorary colonel, E. P. Awdry, formally approached Major-General Sir David Dawnay, a Tenth Hussar who had commanded the North Irish Horse in the war to establish the enduring link to the 10th Royal Hussars (PWO), who also wore the Prince of Wales feathers as a cap badge.

The bar within the drill hall or canteen as it was known in the 1950s was and indeed still is an important meeting place for many yeomen after training nights and parades. The relaxed atmosphere allowed the NCOs and officers to talk to their men and gauge opinion. The name 'drill hall' persisted until the 2000s when TA centre and finally Army Reserve Centre replaced this quaint term.

Brigadier John Platt was the TA Association secretary who would later write the excellent and very readable history of the RWY from 1907–1967. He served with the Somerset Light Infantry (SLI) and was evacuated from Dunkirk; he later served in North Africa, Sicily, and Italy, where he was awarded his DSO. He commanded the SLI as the last British infantry battalion to leave India following partition and was secretary of the Wiltshire TA and Auxiliary forces association for sixteen years, living to be 100 (see p. 187).

Colonel Charles Sivewright MC, the TA Association chairman, served in the Northamptonshire Yeomanry and 11th Hussars (PAO) during the war and

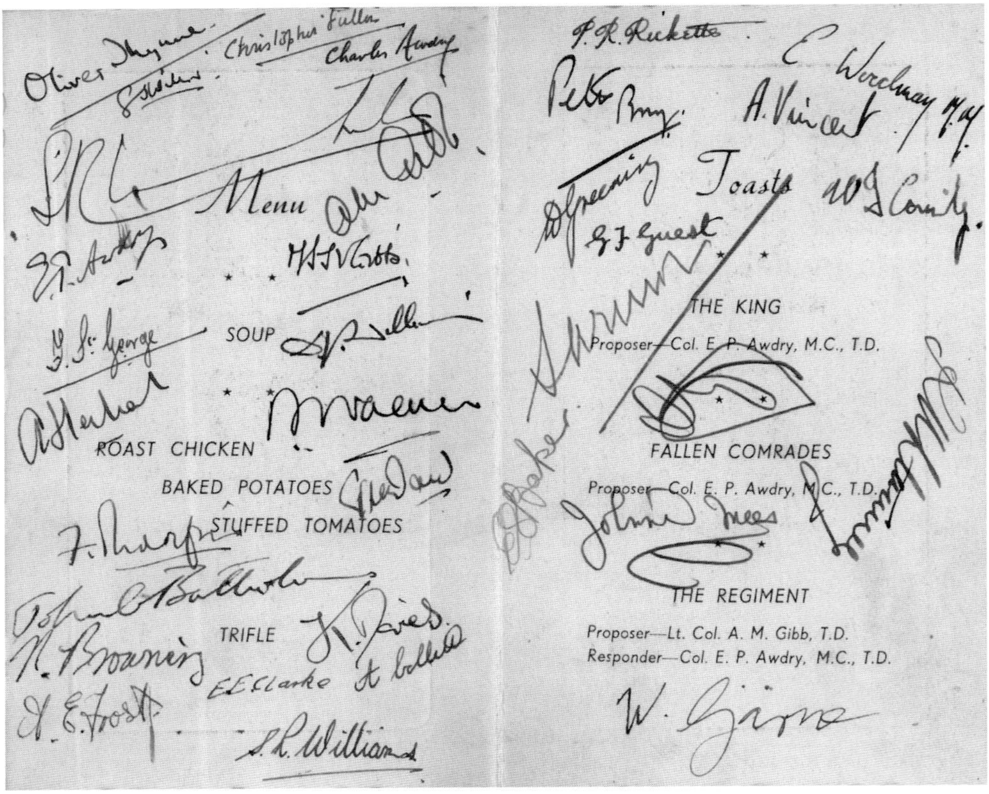

Menu

SOUP

ROAST CHICKEN

BAKED POTATOES

STUFFED TOMATOES

TRIFLE

Toasts

THE KING

Proposer—Col. E. P. Awdry, M.C., T.D.

FALLEN COMRADES

Proposer—Col. E. P. Awdry, M.C., T.D.

THE REGIMENT

Proposer—Lt. Col. A. M. Gibb, T.D.

Responder—Col. E. P. Awdry, M.C., T.D.

The reunion menu from 1947 signed by many prominent wartime yeomen.

'A' Squadron on parade in Salisbury marketplace in 1952 with FV4101 Charioteers and Archer tank destroyers. The Charioteer was a modified Cromwell tank armed with a more powerful 20-pounder gun. As with many modified AFV designs, it had many flaws; the turret was lightly armoured and had a high profile and ammunition stowage within the vehicle was limited. Perhaps more importantly, access to good tank country for heavy armour was very restricted, which led to difficulties with training.

The regiment led the TA contingent on a cold and wet day in June 1953 for the coronation of HM Queen Elizabeth II. *Back Row:* Tpr Clifford, L/Cpl Parsley, Cpl Cooper, Sgt Bowden, Tpr Moore, L/Cpl Bridewell, and Tpr Hallet. *Middle Row:* Sgt Teagle, L/Cpl Merrett, Sgt Holborn, L/Cpl Wilkins, Cpl Austin, Cpl Glover, and Cpl Tremlett. *Front Row:* SQMS Woods, RQMS Hill, Maj. D Mangnall, Lt-Col. T. Gibbs, Capt. D. Awdry, and RQMS Storie.

The opening of the new bar in the Trowbridge drill hall 1957.

thereafter with the Fife and Forfar Yeomanry and Royal Gloucestershire Hussars as commanding officer from 1964–1967.

Conversion to armoured cars took place in 1958 allowing freedom of movement which had previously been extremely difficult with tracked vehicles, but the key event of this year was the Golden Jubilee of the Territorial Army. Three officers and thirty-six other ranks represented the regiment in front of Her Majesty in a very wet Hyde Park.

During the late 1950s, the RWY continued to train and socialise following a pattern that would continue into the early 2000s; however, what is very apparent from studying these halcyon days of soldiering with armoured cars was the very close and symbiotic working relationship that was evolving with the 10th Hussars.

Trooper David Stevens joined the regiment at Devizes in the 1950s (his son, Neil, served in the 1980s) and when interviewed in 2019 David gave his reason for enlistment as simply wanting to learn to drive. He started on a 3-ton Bedford truck in 1957, and it took twelve months to be ready for the test; on the day, there were six candidates in the back of a 1-ton Austin lorry:

> I was driving along and the instructor said to me, what was the sign we just passed. I said what sign? Out, out you've failed. I was so angry that I yanked the yard long hand brake as hard as I could I was in such a temper and I jumped out and got in the back. I could see he driver and instructor struggling with the hand brake and the instructor shouts out Stephens, get up here and get this hand brake off. I immediately shouted back only if you'll let me have another go; and he did and I passed.

Tpr David Stevens.

He recalled the death of George Baker from North Newton, who was standing with him on parade that morning; he 'got into a speed wobble' in a Daimler Dingo armoured car that became uncontrollable, threw him from the vehicle, and then rolled onto him, causing his fatal injuries.

Although he was not personally involved in a training accident, on exercise in Germany in 1968, his troop leader, Lieutenant K. C. Combe, led three Saladin armoured cars down a track that, unbeknown to the following vehicles, was too narrow with a precipitous drop on the right. As the vehicles were unable to move forwards, the crew bailed out, but David was left in the driving seat of the lead vehicle in a convoy that was in retreat with the turret reversed, overhanging the driver's hatch.

The turret had to be turned to allow the driver to escape, but in David's words, 'the silly buggers turned the turret with the barrel down causing the vehicle to slip further towards the edge'. Thankfully, it became lodged or 'bellied' and was recovered by a six-wheel REME Scammel dating from the last war; it was filmed on a cine camera by David, who was fully expecting the vehicle to go over the edge and was keen to capture the incident.

The vehicles had no power steering and were hard work. David remembered the only way to exit the aged Daimler armoured car was through the turret as the driver's vision hatch was far too small. The uncomfortable seat was a piece of canvas stretched across two metal rods. David's memories continue:

> The first job of the day was to go through each gear position and pump the pedal twelve times which was hard work and if you didn't do this, somewhere during the day you would get what you call a false neutral when the lever would all of a sudden shoot back at you and if your foot was on the pedal at the time, your knee would be forced into the steering wheel and you could break your knee.

He described the Saladin as a lovely vehicle to drive that was much more reliable than the Daimlers, but the steering wheel in the Saladin was angled 'upside down', which initially led to great difficulty with overcorrection when trying to keep the vehicle running in a straight line.

All TA units in the county were inspected by the lord-lieutenant, the earl of Pembroke and Montgomery who presented the first of the newly instituted Lord Lieutenant's certificates for service to the TA. The men paraded in battledress and blancoed belts, with the officers in 'blues' with swords, some of which were certainly not regulation pattern. As is often the case, sword drill proved testing for the officers. Lt-Col. Hugh Brassey, the CO, described the pride felt by all as they swung into the market square to the tune of the regiment's quick march, 'God bless the Prince of Wales.'

In the days of horsed cavalry, polo was a popular sport both in India and the UK; the first inter-regimental polo tournament was played in England in 1878. In the 1920s, Tidworth in Wiltshire became and still remains today the centre for military polo. Prior to the Second World War, when there were

Four RWY trumpeters on parade for the opening of the new TA drill hall at Bishopsdown House in Salisbury in 1958.

A joint celebration in the early 1950s with soldiers from the Wiltshire Regiment, the RWY, the 10th Hussars, and a large number of old comrades.

The 1958 Jubilee Parade in Salisbury marketplace. All TA units in the county were inspected by the lord-lieutenant, the earl of Pembroke and Montgomery, who presented the first of the newly instituted lord lieutenant's certificates for service to the TA. The men paraded in battledress and blancoed belts, the officers in 'blues' with swords, some of which were certainly not regulation pattern. As is often the case, sword drill proved testing for the officers. Lt-Col. Hugh Brassey, the CO, described the pride felt by all as they swung into the market square to the tune of 'God bless the Prince of Wales'.

four cavalry regiments in Tidworth, there would be anything up to forty chukkas in a day's polo with six grounds in use.

In 1959, having beaten both the Coldstream and Grenadier Guards, a RWY team overcame the Queen's Own Hussars in the semi-final. A dramatic win against the Royal Horse Guards in the final then marked a unique year for yeomanry polo.

Further success would take another forty years when in the early 1990s, the Royal Wessex Yeomanry won the tournament and again in 2007 and 2008, a year when the RWxY team won all the military polo competitions led by Captain Tim Verdon, a two-goal handicapped Wiltshire Yeoman.

MATCHES SUNDAY, 5TH JULY, 1959

3 p.m. **Semi Final Inter Regimental Tournament**

Queen's Own Hussars (Garter Blue, Red and Gold)		v.	The Royal Wiltshire Yeomanry (Green, Red and Gold)	
1.	Lieut. T. W. Ritson		1.	Major C. P. M. van Limburg Stirum ...
2.	Lieut. C. A. R. Lockhart		2.	Captain C. A. Morrison ... ...
3.	Lieut. M. J. Sherwin		3.	Captain The Hon. G. B. Bathurst ... ...
Bk.	Captain M. Q. Fraser		Bk.	Major M. Watson ... ...

Umpires: Brigadier D. C. Barbour and Squadron-Leader E. C. Roark.
Referee: Brigadier R. W. Hobson.

3.50 p.m. **An Invitation Match**

Canford (Dark Blue)			v.	Fonthill (Green)		
1.	R. Harding	−2		1.	J. I. Morrison	0
2.	P. Coleman	0		2.	Major M. Fox	0
3.	H. R. Kennard	0		3.	Brigadier H. Ley	1
Bk.	Lt.-Colonel G. Spottiswoode	0		Bk.	Major J. G. Morrison	1
		−2				2

Umpires: Brigadier R. W. Hobson and Major H. Hook.

The Final of the Inter Regimental will be played on the Fisher Ground, Tidworth at 3 p.m., Saturday, 11th July, 1959. There will be no Polo on Sunday, 12th July, 1959.

In 1959, having beaten both the Coldstream and Grenadier Guards, a RWY team overcame the Queen's Own Hussars in the semi-final. A dramatic win against the Royal Horse Guards in the final then marked a unique year for yeomanry polo.

Unidentified soldier, Mick Mallon, and Phil Brooks. The Daimler Dingo scout car was a much-loved, fast, four-wheel-drive reconnaissance vehicle that first saw active service in 1940 and continued until it was gradually replaced by the Daimler Ferret in the 1950s.

Lt C. J. Spence, RWY (late 10th Hussars), Sgt Parsley, and Cpl Godfrey (10th Hussars) with the Right Hon. John Profumo MP. The year 1960 was important for the regiment as it avoided amalgamation in the first streamlining of the Territorial Army and saw the presentation of the first Saladin armoured cars to the RWY at the Duke of York's Headquarters in the King's Road, London, by the secretary of state for war, the Right Hon. John Profumo MP—happier times for the minister who himself had been a yeoman, serving with the Northamptonshire Yeomanry in the Second World War Two, before the Profumo Affair became international news.

Colonel Ferris St George, the pre-war adjutant, also ended his tenure as honorary colonel in 1960, but the much-admired Colonel John Morrison was appointed to replace him, continuing the strong family link with two sons both serving in the regiment.

The 1961 Guidon Parade

On 11 June, at Bhutpore Barracks in Tidworth, the regiment paraded in four separate guards under the command of Lt-Col. A. D. S. Magnell TD. Following inspection by the earl of Pembroke, a message from Royal Honorary Colonel HRH the Duke of Windsor was read aloud, expressing his regret at not being able to attend this memorable occasion.

The guidon is presented to Squadron Sergeant-Major E. Ficke by the earl of Pembroke CVO, lord-lieutenant of Wiltshire, with Sgts P. Tremlett and W. Jaques forming the escort on either side.

The earl of Pembroke and RWY Honorary Colonel Lord Margadale inspect the parade. The ramrod straight trooper talking to The Earl had previously served in the Life Guards. Behind the commanding officer, Lt-Col. Derek Magnall, is the Regimental 2IC Maj. Mike Watson MC, who had previously served with the 17th/21st Lancers and would become the next commanding officer.

Above: Lt Anthony Pitt-Rivers from the well-known Dorset family and founders of the Pitt-Rivers Museum in Oxford on the left of the turret.

Below: 'A' Squadron Saladin armoured cars at Lulworth Ranges in 1963 with the troop leader Lt Peter Calver a veterinary surgeon and well-known racehorse trainer standing right of picture. Each squadron spent three days at Lulworth in Dorset. The gunnery was a success as described in the formal report:

> The firing programme was well organised and carried out, the shooting was good by any standards. The Regiment showed great keenness and were quite obviously determined to do well.

Above: A road traffic accident involving a Saladin armoured car at Downton, 1962. The FV601 Saladin armoured car had a long and protracted development history, finally entering service in 1959. The main armament was a 76-mm gun; with a crew of three and a road speed of 45 mph, it acted as both a reconnaissance vehicle and a wheeled tank but was eventually replaced by the much lighter and tracked FV101 Scorpion.

Many drivers reported that if a wheel was caught in a verge or curb, the Saladin could be pulled violently off the road. At annual camp in Yorkshire in June 1962, due to pooling of vehicles from the Westminster Dragoons and the North Irish Horse, the RWY was able to deploy with a regiment's worth of armoured cars. However, the weather was appalling, and one troop leader managed to destroy 100 yards of a solid Yorkshire stone wall with his Saladin; he was reported to have ordered the wall to fall down after the first stone was dislodged. The year 1962 also saw the establishment of the short-lived TA emergency reserve, which acquired the name 'the Ever-Readies' and, as the name suggests, were on a much shorter notice to mobilise.

Opposite: The mayor of Salisbury visits the squadron in 1963 to present the annual TA bounty of £150 to Cpl Owen and Sgt Pidgley. Although still an attractive tax-free bonus, the reserve soldier is generally not driven by financial compensation for the many evenings and weekends spent away from his or her family.

07C

Saladin armoured cars in the Wylye Valley 1963. Of note is the variety of uniform worn by the officers—a characteristic trait within the yeomanry as a whole. Lt J. Chetwode and Lt H. Sykes discuss tactics with Capt. N. Delmaine, 2IC 'A' Squadron.

Opposite above: The RWY and the 10th Hussars provided a guard for the first showing of Daryl Zannuck's classic war movie *The Longest Day*, screened at the Gaumont cinema in Frome in 1962. The local newspaper quoted the lord lieutenant of Somerset being delayed 'due to a misunderstanding about the date'.

Opposite below: The 1964 rifle meeting, Bulford. Cpl Bruton is the regimental individual winner. The importance of accurate marksmanship for a cavalry soldier became more relevant when a support troop was formed in 1964. These soldiers, carried by Alvis Saracen six-wheeled armoured personnel carriers, were trained to hold ground taken by the armoured cars and received specialist infantry and explosives training. The annual rifle meeting was for decades an important regimental event.

THE LONGEST DAY
DARRYL F. ZANUCK'S THE LONGEST DAY
TODAY

As 1967 dawned, the RWY once again faced possible disbandment under a Labour government defence review that had been announced two years previously. The Territorial Army formed in 1908 was to be renamed the Territorial and Army Volunteer Reserve (TAVR), and the surviving elements of the RWY would become a squadron of the newly formed Royal Yeomanry Regiment; also, a company of the Royal Wiltshire Territorials who were disbanded only eighteen months later. The complex defence reviews which involved rebranding, and reallocation of those wearing the three feathers cap badge, would continue for another fifty years.

Presentation of medals by Colonel Lord Margadale of Islay in 1967. John Morrison served in the RWY during the war before becoming the MP for Salisbury in 1942. He became chairman of the powerful Conservative 1922 Committee and was thought to be responsible for Edward Heath becoming prime minister. The photograph shows him as honorary colonel presenting TA efficiency medals to members of HQ Squadron at Fonthill near Tisbury. He is accompanied by the commanding officer, Robert Heywood-Lonsdale MC, formerly of the Grenadier Guards, who was the last CO of the RWY as a complete regiment.

10

'A' (RWY) Squadron, The Royal Yeomanry

The Royal Yeomanry Regiment, the first of the new yeomanry regiments, was formed in 1967 and was allocated a NATO role in the British Army of the Rhine. Major-General Sir Desmond Rice KCVO, CBE, serving with 1st Queen's Dragoon Guards, described those early years:

> I was sitting at my desk in Berlin when I was told that I was to command a T and AVR regiment.
>
> Abbreviations have never meant much to me and this one was certainly meaningless. Eventually, I heard that the Regiment was to be formed on the 1st April 1967 and to be called The Royal Yeomanry Regiment and it was to consist of five squadrons each drawn from an existing yeomanry regiment. A light aid detachment and a band were yet to be formed.
>
> The problems that beset me as the first Commanding Officer were legion. The first thing was to get to know everyone, not an easy task when I was only able to get around the squadrons one weekend in every six. The second was to set realistic targets. If the best people were to stay, all of whom were busy in civilian life, it was important not to set a pace which would drive them out. At the same time, we were being carefully watched. For many were sceptical that we could look after all our equipment and train to the same standard as an armoured recce regiment in the Regular Army.
>
> After a busy first year, I was allowed to take half the regiment to Germany for camp, with the promise that I could take the other half the following year. After much argument, we were allowed to drive our vehicles with crew to the port of embarkation. We had to let the tyres of the Ferrets down to get them into the overhead gantries, while all the civilian cars and buses had to wait until all our vehicles were loaded, much to the amazement and to some annoyance for those who found there was no room for them.

> After crossing to Bremerhaven, we then drove on to Wolfenbuttel, an excellent mobilisation exercise in itself. I knew how important the first camp in Germany would be. We would be watched to see whether we were good enough to do our job on mobilisation.

He continues:

> I once saw two Saladins and two Ferret scout cars being filled up at a BP filling station, so I stopped and asked the troop leader (Lord Shelbourne) why on earth he was using his personal credit card to pay a vast fuel bill instead of asking for some fuel to be sent up. His reply was 'Oh Colonel there is so much to remember, this way seems much easier'. Needless to say, his troop would have followed him anywhere out of interest to see what was going to happen next!
>
> A Lt General, the General Officer Commanding, was visiting a squadron one weekend. The troop in question was on a river, in a position of observation with a Ferret forward and the rest of the vehicles in a hide to the rear. We arrived on the riverbank to be met by the troop leader (who could have done with a haircut). When asked why the two men were not dug in; the troop leader replied 'If you were a farmer, you would not take kindly to having holes dug on your land.' We then went into the hide where the troop sergeant stood up and gave a magnificent salute (he had been in the Grenadier Guards). The general said 'Why aren't you lying down.'
>
> The sergeant replied 'I normally stand up when talking to generals, but if you wish me to lie down sir, I will.' Not my day as I found out later.

The 1969 training based in Germany with 5RTR had many sceptics and some of the more critical wondered how many vehicles would be left behind in Germany. Two days were spent moving overseas on HMS *Sir Percival* in an era when many of these Wiltshire soldiers may have never left the UK, so the sea voyage itself for many was a great experience.

An important aspect to the training and recruiting year at this time (when the public may have been under the impression that the reserve forces had been disbanded) was the presence of the recruiting team from Swindon at fetes, flower shows, and other events throughout the county.

Major David Part handed over command of 'A' Squadron to Major Kenneth Combe, an insurance broker in 1970. In October that year, the army decided that TAVR officers should take a promotion exam that was 'special to arm', which resulted in a degree of consternation with comments such as 'never heard of such a thing', 'I do it only as a hobby', and 'resigning tomorrow'. The exam was run from the old Royal Hussars mess at Perham Down with copious quantities of brandy and ginger ale available to 'keep out the cold'.

The year 1977 saw the departure of the last Saladin armoured car following years of loyal service and the arrival of Fox armoured cars, requiring nine consecutive weekends of intensive conversion training. June marked HM the Queen's Silver Jubilee and 'A' Squadron was represented by Corporal Pound

Lt-Col. Part receiving the Burberry trophy from Prime Minister Heath during Exercise London Pride, 1972. The trophy was awarded for best recruiting poster submitted by a TAVR unit. Part served as a national service officer with the 17th/21st Lancers, joining the RWY in 1952. He was one of the three officers present in Hyde Park for the Golden Jubilee of the TA and was on parade in 1961 for the presentation of the guidon. He was the first squadron leader of the newly formed RWY Squadron of the Royal Yeomanry and later commanded the Royal Yeomanry from 1971–1973 while running the General Trading Company in Sloane Square. He was appointed honorary colonel of the RWY in 1988 and is one of the few who have an encyclopaedic memory of the regiment, spanning six decades.

and Lance Corporals Lake and Quince at a royal review of the reserve forces at Wembley.

In 1978, the last of the Fullers and Bartholomews left the RWY, and the squadron deployed again to Germany exercising firstly in the Cuxhaven region in the north, much of which was below sea level and very wet, then onwards to Paderborn. Although forty years later, overseas training is a routine part of reserve service, this was not the case in the 1970s when only a proportion of the TA had a defined NATO role.

The predictable pattern of events continued into the early 1980s with inspections, trade, troop training, and gunnery and regimental exercises at weekends, but the highlight of the training year was always the two weeks annual camp with the hope of living up to the Royal Yeomanry recruitment slogan of the era who admitted to 'getting it at weekends', perhaps most appropriate when in Hamburg in 1978 rather than on Salisbury Plain.

'Crusader 80' was the codename for three interconnected exercises in 1980—Exercise Square Leg was held in the UK; Exercise Jog-Trot involved the movement of UK forces to West Germany; and Exercise Spearpoint was the field training

Cpl Mitchell and Tpr Collins from support troop 'de-bus' from a camouflaged FV603 Saracen armoured personnel carrier.

Lt Robert Floyd and Terry Hart—marvellous images from a different era; the haircuts, the weapons, and the headgear.

exercise itself in Germany. With lines of communication and resupply stretching back to the UK, Crusader was the largest NATO exercise to date, held south of Hannover, involving three armoured divisions and the mobilisation of 20,000 soldiers from the TA.

The deployment of the TA contingent began as with any exercise on the evening of Friday 12 September with long vehicle columns heading towards the east coast ports in the UK. The squadron with the addition of sixteen Wiltshire yeomen from the Royal Wessex Yeomanry deployed from Sennelager in central Germany with two troops attached to the 9th/12th Lancers and two detached to the 5th Battalion Royal Anglian Regiment. This exercise took two years to plan and cost approximately £8 million but allowed the British Army to practise at corps level and the rapid reinforcement of the BAOR in time of crisis.

As 1980 came to a close, Squadron Sergeant-Major Harry Garlick, one of the stalwarts of the yeomanry, left Swindon to take up the non-regular permanent staff (NRPS) post in 'B' Squadron, where he continued to serve the RWY for many years.

The early years of the 1980s also saw the departure of many stout yeomen who had served both the squadron and, for some, the squadron bar for two decades or more. Lieutenant Roger Field joined the squadron in 1983, a notable officer as he was a rarity having had war fighting experience from his time in the Blues and Royals in the Falklands Conflict of 1982. In later years, he would write *Rogue Male*, the excellent biography of an officer from the Royal Gloucestershire Hussars who was as renowned for his seduction skills as well as his talent on the battlefield. Major James Arkell also arrived to take the helm at Swindon; he would later command his regiment and be appointed honorary colonel of the RWY. As a squadron leader, he was keen to name training exercises after beer and brewing including Exercise Mash Tun and Grist Case.

There was a significant difference between overseas training in Germany, which was focused on field training, and the UK camps of the 1980s in Westdown on Salisbury Plain and Castlemartin in Pembrokeshire, which inevitably included the delights of guard duty, fatigues, drill parades, and subaltern's inspections. Strangely enough, two weeks of pure soldiering proved far more popular.

The year 1984 saw the arrival of tracked CVR(T) to replace the wheeled Saracen armoured personnel carriers and the joys of BATCO, a term now unfamiliar to the modern digital soldier. It was a form of secure and encoded communication involving a plastic wallet and sheets of numbers and letters.

WO2 Fred Feltham, who served with the Eleventh and then the Royal Hussars, took over as permanent staff instructor (PSI) squadron sergeant-major in Swindon and continues to work at the time of writing; a keen photographer, he meticulously catalogued the historical collection for the author.

The high point of the year was another large NATO exercise in mainland Europe—Exercise Lionheart. 'A' Squadron formed part of the UK 2nd Division fighting as NATO's Blue Army in a series of parallel exercises along the inner German border and stretching into Denmark and Norway.

The journey to Sennelager was itself a trial of endurance, involving, for many, cattle trucks and ninety crewmen spending twenty-four hours in a railway carriage designed for sixty. The first week was spent as rear area security (a classic yeomanry task), but in week two, the serious business of forward reconnaissance was tested 150 miles to the east. Trooper Mark Godard of Swindon became a real casualty when he was hit in the mouth by a rifle butt from a rather enthusiastic TA paratrooper from 10 Para at RAF Gutersloh; by the end of the day, both sides were throwing bricks at each other.

Throughout the mid- to late 1980s, the years passed as they had for generations before; the high turnover within the TA and limited training time was possibly one of the reasons the squadron adjutant was heard to utter in his sleep at night 'but we did it like this last year' while banging his head against the ground.

The Royal Yeomanry was the only TA unit allocated to the international training Exercise Certain Shield in 1991, acting as enemy under the command of a Dutch brigade to the newly formed multinational airmobile division. The strong performance in the field and at gunnery camp, together with vigorous lobbying of the army board, were factors in the survival of the squadron in the Royal Yeomanry ORBAT following the defence review 'Options for Change', which brought with it a new role of national defence reconnaissance for the Eastern District.

Captain (later Colonel) Toby Bridge KRH, a Wiltshire man with an unsurpassed knowledge of RWY history, left the squadron in 1994 following his posting as the last regular adjutant, and with his departure, the affiliation to the KRH changed as conversion to a chemical reconnaissance regiment took place.

An increase in the number of attached regular instructors from the Royal Tank Regiment and conversion to Fuchs crewmen began in earnest in 1995 when the PSIs returned from their training course in Alabama. Training was now focused on the use of the mobile mass spectrometer for chemical sampling from the vehicle and the basics of NBC (nuclear, biological, and chemical) reconnaissance, a skill that was still being used by 'B' Squadron at that time but with far less sophisticated equipment—essentially hand-held rods mounting chemical detection paper.

Major Dominic Guinness took command of the squadron in 2001, a year when annual training took place in Egypt as part of the United Kingdom's contribution to a major US exercise. The exercise took place a few weeks after the attacks on the World Trade Centre in New York, and it became apparent to the yeomen that the world had changed as a live air defence battery was placed around the exercising troops.

Tpr Lee wearing an early pattern dark green NBC suit and armed with a L4A4 light machine gun, the successor to the Bren gun during Exercise Lionheart, 1984.

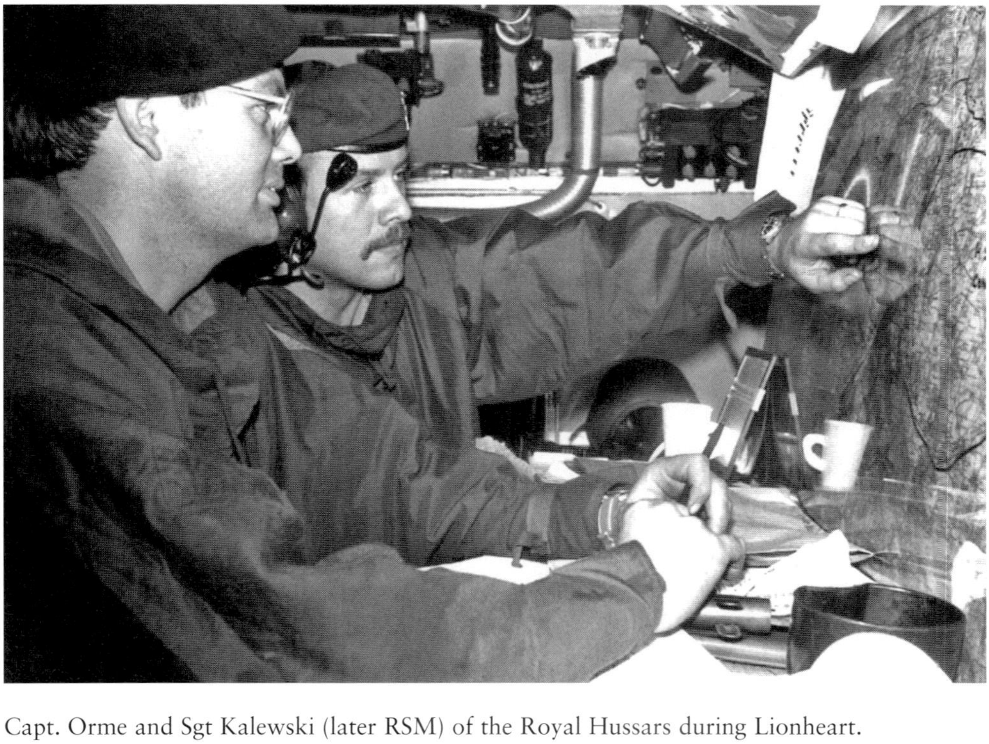

Capt. Orme and Sgt Kalewski (later RSM) of the Royal Hussars during Lionheart.

Squadron Fox armoured car commander plan their route, with Kevin Carter, Neville Mullings, and Lt George Windsor Clive, who had previously served in the Coldstream Guards.

Left to right: The troop leader Lt Cook, Sgt Shaun Collins, and an exercise umpire. The Fox was notoriously top-heavy, and this sort of incident was always a risk on exercise. Neil Stevens was at the wheel of this particular vehicle in Gehrden, West Germany, in 1986 and recalled his commander reading a gentleman's illustrated magazine to him to keep him awake when driving and presumed he must have been distracted by the photographs in the article and momentarily stopped.

The vehicle was eventually recovered by the REME whose Samson tracked recovery vehicle threw a track in the adjacent ploughed field much to the amusement of the Fox crew and passing children.

Fighting vehicle 721 Fox (FV721) was designed in the early 1960s as a replacement for the Ferret armoured car. Powered by a 4.2-litre Jaguar petrol engine, it had excellent road performance and the ability to cross most types of terrain. At its peak, the Royal Yeomanry had eighty vehicles, each armed with a 30-mm Rarden cannon.

Maj. Robert Sutcliffe (centre), who served as a regular cavalry officer with the 14th/20th King's Hussars, commanded the Royal Yeomanry, rising to the rank of brigadier and served as honorary colonel of the RWY. Cpl Stokes is left of picture and Ben Merrett right in coveralls in a classic Cold War tank commander's uniform.

A recruitment drive outside an Ushers pub, a Trowbridge-based Wiltshire brewery between 1824 and 2000, with Cpl Mortimer, Cpl Goodhead, Sgt Margetts, Cpl Carson, and Tpr Lewis. Cpl (later S/Sgt) 'Murph' Carson was born in Dublin in 1949 and joined the Royal Ulster Rifles in 1967, which, following amalgamation, became the Royal Irish Rangers, with whom he served as a regular soldier until 1975.

He joined the Royal Yeomanry in Trowbridge and served from 1980 until 2014, including a tour of Iraq aged fifty-four. He still works part time at 'Y' Squadron RWxY in Swindon, marking forty-seven years as a soldier.

Ben Merritt, a popular troop leader in the early 1990s, who went on to become a successful CEO in industry, and S/Sgt Jimmy Walters. The young boy had been seriously ill and had a wonderful private tour of the tank park.

The honorary colonel, David Part, receives the freedom of Trowbridge from the mayor, Councillor Mr J. G. Attenburrow in July 1989; this was the first civic honour granted by a Wiltshire town since the 1940s. A mounted drive-past the old town hall was followed by a march-past of an impressive contingent from the RWY old comrades.

Eccentricity among yeomanry officers (and, to a lesser extent, regular cavalry officers) was commonplace, and in the 1990s, it was not unusual to see a private vehicle on a weekend exercise. There were logistical reasons behind this practice, as officers frequently travelled long distances to attend training on a Friday evening. A Range Rover fitted with a Clansman radio was, however, a slightly more unusual sight even in 1992.

There was much discussion on this very wet exercise as to whether a sheep could be deposited into the vehicle at night unnoticed by the owner. This was a welcome distraction from the chef's curry he produced for five consecutive nights leading to a sense of humour failure and loss of morale among some yeomen.

The late Capt. Philip Ashton- Johnson, known affectionately as 'AJ', right of picture who has clearly forgotten his 'boots combat high' for the weekend exercise. Rory Stewart in *The Prince of the Marshes* recalls meeting him in Iraq: 'This was AJ, currently in charge of CPA finances. He was a Territorial cavalry officer and the only man dressed in civilian clothes'. The yeomanry as a whole had many such charismatic and loyal characters, displaying eccentricities of dress and mannerism, adding a sense of style and fun to soldiering.

The TPz (*Transportpanzer*) Fuchs NBC reconnaissance vehicle. During the First Gulf War, coalition forces found themselves lacking a specialised, mobile, nuclear, and chemical detection force. Unable to send troops, Germany contributed sixty of these 6 × 6 vehicles. Thereafter, this capability was assigned to the Royal Yeomanry and 'A' Squadron, allowing mobile analysis and marking of potentially contaminated ground.

Exercise Bright Star in Egypt, 2001. WO2 Pulford and Sgt Woods at Alamein Camp in the Egyptian desert wearing temperate pattern DPM camouflage.

Operation Telic, 2003

Lt-Col. (later Major-General) Simon Brooks-Ward took command of the Royal Yeomanry in 2002, and Iraq was very much a discussion point from the time he was appointed. In December that year, he attended a meeting with fifteen other TA commanding officers and recalled: 'The chairman went around the table and said to everyone you may be going but when addressing them he announced, you are definitely going. It was a bit of wake-up call'.

Major Dominic Guinness recalled that as the autumn of 2002 progressed, nothing was heard from the chain of command, suggesting mobilisation was a possibility, but on 20 December, the commanding officer called him into his office in Olympia, where he was running the International Horse of the Year Show and announced that the RY would be forming a composite squadron to be mobilised in the New Year. Dominic was told he could discuss this with no one but addressed the squadron in the bar in Swindon on the final drill night before Christmas, suggesting 'they make no medium term plans, book no holidays, get life sorted and take some more exercise. Most got the message'.

> Following a surreal conversation with my employer along the lines of what would happen if..., Christmas passed in a blur and planning started in earnest but the pace was about to increase when the Chief of Staff Royal Armoured Corps started a meeting stating that The Royal Yeomanry would move from 180 days' notice to move to fourteen!

S/Sgt Wadsworth REME, WO2 SSM Pulford, and WO2 RQMS Walters undergoing pre-deployment training at a chilly Knook Camp in Wiltshire. The two warrant officers later changed roles in Kuwait.

The yeomen gathered at the mobilisation centre in Chilwell in Nottinghamshire, not far from their predecessors in 1939, and was joined by thirty drivers from the Royal Logistic Corps (160 Regiment RLC), who were required to drive the IMMLC trucks that carried the decontamination equipment. Within three days of arrival at Knook Camp in Wiltshire for familiarisation training, the large vehicle convoy of over fifty vehicles was taken away to Marchwood Military Port in Southampton and a short four-day package of training (including bayonet fighting) was hastily put together.

The advance party left for the desert in mid-February and the remainder of the yeoman were granted a week's leave before waiting at RHQ in London to be deployed. The general returned to his own recollections:

> 1RTR requested 115 personnel and were initially very sceptical that we would get the people and secondly, be able to provide the capability. I had no doubts and when the call went out in January 2003, 133 volunteered with the majority coming from the RWY. They never disappointed; led by Dominic Guinness, the composite squadron enlarged and was called Y (Yeomanry) Squadron. They were deployed as the decontamination squadron for 1 RTR and I was detached to the US Exploitation Task Force (75th XTF) with my RHQ and echelon that included several RWY members including Captains Richard Nall and the late and much-loved Captain Bob Guillou.

The general continued:

> Bob to me was the epitome of a Wiltshire Yeoman; his Wiltshire burr, his sense of humour and his determination to be mobilised demonstrated all the Wiltshire Yeomanry qualities.
>
> At the end of the tour I remember getting our first shower in Kuwait; I stood next to Bob and looked down to see his false teeth on display, he must have been one of the oldest men deployed.

Expecting a chemical hazard, the squadron was split throughout the deployed UK Division. An augmented section (section-plus) commanded by Second Lieutenant Conn MacEvilly was sent to 'G' Squadron of the Joint NBC Regiment (JNBCR) who would protect 16 Air Assault Brigade during its move into Iraq. Although serving as a Westminster Dragoon, Conn went on to command the Wiltshire squadron and then the Royal Yeomanry.

Second Lieutenant Mike Dalzell from 'A' Squadron deployed with a section-plus to Camp Viking to provide decontamination capability for the Royal Marines. Mike would later command the squadron and was the last RY squadron leader before the Swindon squadron was allocated to the RWxY.

Lieutenant Simon Keyes, also a Royal Wiltshire Yeoman, deployed with two sections to reinforce 'D' Squadron of the JNBCR, who would accompany 7 Armoured Brigade. Trooper (later Sergeant) Mark Denman, who had joined the RWY in 2000 and served in Kosovo in 2001, described to the author his experience of mobilisation:

> I was working late at Wiltshire College in Chippenham and was in a meeting when the college receptionist interrupted and said I had an important phone call; it was my troop sergeant asking where I was. At this point I had not received my mobilisation papers, and I spoke to my boss and told him I needed to leave work immediately, arriving at the squadron at about 21.00 to a hive of excitement and activity. The next day my employer asked if he should appeal against the decision as there was an OFSTED inspection looming and the students were then told that I had been mobilised. I told them they had nine days to get their completed assignments in and to my surprise, all of them achieved this.
>
> On my final day, as I entered the class room all the students were there to say good bye. On the wall was a six foot sheet of paper they had prepared with the words 'please don't die'; other comments included 'shoot one in the butt for me' and 'if you die can I have your car.'

Second Lieutenant (now Lieutenant-Colonel) Conn MacEvilly, a London barrister, who would go on to command 'A' Squadron and subsequently the RY, described the entry into Iraq:

> The day of the ground assault came. As the coalition forces advanced, we passed trigger points at which it was expected that chemical or biological weapons would be used against us. It was daunting to know in advance each time that a threshold of that sort was about to be crossed, given what our job would have been if we had faced retaliation. But although we had many such moments, the direst news never came.

Like the Royal Wiltshire Yeomanry in the First World War, the deployed reservists were eventually re-tasked as infantry following the fall of Baghdad, assisting in peace support operations around Basra, returning to the UK in May. Major-General Brooks-Ward recalls the return to the UK:

> On our return, the Squadron got itself back together in a very short time. We have to remember that at the time we were guinea-pigs with no mission specific training. We self-trained at Knook Camp and we only gave the soldiers two weeks to get their world affairs in order. The strength of the Squadron lies in its history, heritage and the uplifting togetherness of the rank and file. It was tested and not found wanting.

In 2005, the Royal Yeomanry received the first battle honour awarded to the Territorial Army since the Second World War for its efforts in Iraq during major combat operations between the 19 March and 30 April 2003. The citation for the award praises the personnel of the Royal Yeomanry for their 'utmost steadfastness and gallantry in the face of hostile fire'.

The RWY elements of the composite squadron continued the tradition of their forefathers from the campaign in the Western Desert of naming vehicles. 2Lt Mike Dalzell with his vehicle *The Prince of Wales*.

Sgt Massey impersonating a well-known local personality.

WO2 Pulford with a group of happy, local children.

The squadron lost Fuchs in 1999 with the creation of the Joint NBC Regiment from 1RTR and 27 Squadron RAF Regiment, and the Prince of Wales feathers was replaced as a cap badge in Sennelager in 2006 when the RY as a whole, re-badged.

In 2007, the Royal Yeomanry's role changed to Formation CBRN Reconnaissance and then finally Formation Reconnaissance in 2009. The role was now to provide individual reinforcements to the Joint CBRN Regiment, but as with every reserve unit, reinforcements were supplied for ongoing operations.

Corporal James Dunsby was one of the many who served on operational tours and was attached to HRH Prince Harry's troop in the Household Cavalry Regiment on Op Herrick 6. James was a member of 'C' Squadron at the time but transferred to 'A' Squadron RY in 2010; in July 2013, he died during SAS selection.

Throughout the entire period during which the RY was involved with Fuchs and to a much lesser extent CVR(T) Spartan, the primary training platform was still the Land Rover until 2011 when training on RWMIK (revised weapons mounted installation kit) Land Rovers started as part of the RY's new role as a lightly armoured but highly mobile, light cavalry regiment supporting 1st Queen's Dragoon Guards.

Afghanistan

Sergeant Mark Denman described his experience as a lance corporal in Afghanistan in 2006:

> I felt I needed a career break. I had a chat with my PSAO and made it clear that if I were mobilised, I wouldn't appeal. Sure enough, a few weeks later the brown envelope landed on my door step signalling another two weeks of excited preparation.
>
> This tour was different again, we had mobilised in time to attend build up training with C Squadron of the Household Cavalry Regiment at a time when the army had now moved from Clansman to Bowman radios and I had not been trained on Bowman. A communication error meant I was assigned to be taught to drive CVR(T) s and did not attend a Bowman course.
>
> It was during this time in Windsor another reservist from the RY identified that I was gay. He promised to keep it secret, and he did, but a rumour spread that one of the reservists was a homosexual.
>
> My initial role was as a driver but our vehicle developed a fuel leak and I was transferred to Rainbow 13, the nickname Rainbow was given as this vehicle already had a gay crew member. I was selected because they thought it needed a bit more straightness. After a few days with the crew I came out, to the dismay of the rest of the troop. Other than the initial surprise at having two thirds of a crew that way inclined the Squadron was very supportive with the sergeant-major even giving me a copy of *Gay Times*.
>
> About two weeks into the first mobile operating group (MOG), we had stopped on an exposed patch of ground whilst support troop checked the route for IEDs. After about ten minutes our commander became a little anxious that we were static for too long and we did indeed come under RPG attack. Being the first attack there was a bit of confusion but by the time the commander said go, I was already halfway up the hill.
>
> For the second MOG I was back into SHQ driving the Sultan. Due to the dust we had to regularly bang out the air filters or the engines would lose power. The convoy had now stopped and I took the opportunity to clear the filter; hatch open, unscrew several bolts and dismantle half of the air intake system. As I was happily knocking out the sand, I noticed the sand near me was splashing. It took a few moments to realise we were under small arms fire and I threw that air filter into the side bin and grabbed a fresh one. It's surprising how quickly I could fit an air filter when the need arose.
>
> We eventually returned to Camp Bastion and from there we flew to Kandahar while we waited about a week before returning to the UK via Cyprus to 'decompress' with enforced fun. It didn't slip my notice that whilst we were being allowed to drink alcohol for the first time in months that the numerous support staff were informally asking questions as to our wellbeing.
>
> Having been outed on my return, which to be honest I feared more than being shot, I was able to participate in the 2008 London *Gay Pride* march as a uniformed

> member of the Army Reserve; my fears about coming out were unfounded, as half of the squadron had already guessed.

In 2012, ten years following the granting of the freedom of Swindon, the squadron, now wearing the cap badge of the Royal Yeomanry, marched through the town. Perhaps more importantly, this parade also celebrated the seventieth anniversary of the Second Battle of El Alamein. On arrival at the civic offices, the military covenant was signed in the council chamber demonstrating Swindon's continued support for the RWY.

From 2011 onwards, a period of intense training followed, which provided a number of challenges, but the squadron rose to the occasion, swelling numbers, and even establishing a troop outpost at Combermere Barracks in Windsor. However, by 2014, the future of 'A' Squadron was in doubt and the option proposed under the Army 2020 restructuring was to withdraw them from the order of battle (less a single troop outpost of 'C' Squadron, the Royal Wessex Yeomanry). The squadron was incredulous at this news and Major (now Lieutenant-Colonel) Mike Dalzell recalls:

> At the time of the announcement, we had around one hundred yeomen on our books, and prided ourselves in having made further progress in training our WMIK crews than the remainder of the Regiment; we simply couldn't believe that the Army would even contemplate this level of self-harm.
>
> Reminding myself that the Squadron and its RWY forebearers had endured tougher times than this over three centuries; I resolved that this would not be the end, and asked my yeomen to believe likewise and continue the fight with me. In the end, the fight paid off—and as will be seen the entire squadron survived as an independent sub-unit as Y (RWY) Squadron The Royal Wessex Yeomanry.

11

'B' (RWY) Squadron, The Royal Wessex Yeomanry

In 1970, a new government led to the decision to increase the size of the reserve element of the British Army, and a second squadron of RWY was raised as part of a new regiment, the Wessex Yeomanry, the 'Royal' prefix being granted later in 1979. Like many other yeomanry regiments, the name, property, and tradition of the RWY had been kept alive by a small cadre, which included Major J. M. Adeley, who had previously served with the North Irish Horse and would later take up the position of second in command of this new regiment, and Captain Alaistair Forbes, an ex-regular Guards officer.

The RWY would serve alongside the Royal Devon Yeomanry and the Royal Gloucestershire Hussars, the RWY having links with the latter dating back to the western desert in the 1940s. Many of the old TA drill halls had, however, been sold, but Bishopsdown House in Salisbury was offered as the squadron's new home, although it was in a rather sorry state.

The first annual camp was in the now derelict New Zealand Camp on Salisbury Plain with the regiment under the command of a Royal Gloucestershire Hussar, Lt-Col. Tom Ponsonby, whose son, Rupert, later the 7th Lord de Mauley, would command the regiment and become colonel commandant of the Yeomanry and honorary colonel of the RWxY.

Health and safety and AFV qualifications were clearly less of an issue in the 1970s as a squadron of tanks and armoured personnel carriers was borrowed for this exercise from the Royal Hussars. Recruitment for this newly formed squadron was encouraging, and by 1972, there were eighty-three all ranks on the books, although an attempt to form a troop in Devizes failed as the local infantry unit had too strong a presence in the area. For the remainder of the 1970s, 'B' Squadron exercised like infantry but without the expertise of the infantry permanent staff.

UK training areas familiar to generations of yeomen are inevitably cold and windswept and hence the opportunity to take part in an overseas deployment so familiar to the Royal Yeomanry was firmly grasped in 1978 when Exercise Copper Beech saw a composite troop deploy to Gibraltar. The 'B' Squadron troop provided the first ever TA guard to the Convent, the governor's residence, requiring precision drill and immaculate uniforms.

The addition of the 'Royal' prefix in 1979 required a parade that was inspected by the duke of Beaufort, who represented HM the Queen. The yeomanry drill was of a surprisingly high standard, and over 1,000 guests attended the parade at Knook Camp in Wiltshire, the officers dining that night at Bowood House, home of the marquess of Lansdowne. The drill of the attached US National Guard was, however, described as 'beyond redemption'.

The welcome transition to a home defence light reconnaissance regiment mounted in Land Rovers took place in 1981; the mission was to provide reconnaissance for the United Kingdom Land Force districts in time of war, but perhaps more importantly, restoring the mounted ethos of the volunteer cavalry. The national recession, however, brought the RWxY to a standstill due to punitive restrictions on the training budget, but a further visit to Gibraltar and the publication of the *Historical Journal of the RWxY* by Major Jeremy Bastin, 'B' Squadron leader and an acclaimed military author—a rather underwhelming year in the history of the reserve forces and this type of scenario would repeat itself in decades to come as uncertainty and lack of finances were now a regular threat.

Annual camp in the early 1970s. Service dress would slowly disappear over the next two decades; numerous excuses were given, but as with many issues in the TA, rather cynically, it may just have been too much effort.

Images from the 1970s—a variety of uniforms, rather large berets, and some fine displays of Victorian facial hair.

Right: This photograph appeared on the cover of the TAVR magazine, entitled 'Brothers in Arms'. Two 'B' Squadron brothers, Peter and Michael Dicker, at Penhale Camp in April 1972 wearing olive green denims and ammunition boots.

Below: Winners of the Wessex Tankard at the South West District Rifle meeting in 1976—Tpr Hemmings, Cpl Wright, Cpl Denham, and Tpr Hoskins.

Lt Terry Arden, with a haircut compatible with the mid-1970s, sends a report to squadron headquarters on the unreliable Pye Westminster radio, which was described by Capt. Richard Jenkins (the HQ troop leader) as 'not soldier proof and quite impractical for use when mobile or in the field'.

Standing with his SLR in the high port is Cpl Price. His son, Wayne, served in the King's Royal Hussars and was a PSI to the Royal Wessex Yeomanry; he continues to serve as the PSAO in Cirencester. He is an accomplished military historian.

WO2 Dawson and his son. 'Nobby' joined the squadron as a staff sergeant instructor from the affiliated regular regiment, the Royal Hussars (PWO), in 1971.

The pattern of life in the Royal Wessex Yeomanry remained unchanged throughout the late 1970s and 1980s. The regiment was administered from RHQ in Cirencester with three squadrons in Gloucestershire, one in Wiltshire, and one in Devon. The squadron identities remained strong, and loyalty was undoubtedly to the original cap badge and not the new regiment. Looking back at this period, there were certainly opportunities to achieve greater military and social cohesion, which did not happen. Colonel John Peel, the honorary colonel to the RWY, described in the 1980 publication *The Historical Journal of The Royal Wessex Yeomanry* the quandary faced by a new recruit who has to absorb the difficult concept of joining two families—his regimental family and the RWY family.

In 1986, the squadron occupied the newly converted TA centre in Old Sarum, which had previously been an RAF station and recruitment started for 'E' (HSF) Squadron. The Home Service Force was an unusual unit administered by the RWxY but more akin to the Home Guard of the last war, whose function was static guard duty at key installations in time of war. The concept died a death in 1992, and many of these senior soldiers transferred directly into 'B' Squadron giving sterling service over a period of many years.

Lt-Col. Oliver Chamberlain handed over command of the Royal Wessex Yeomanry to Lt-Col. Godfrey Tilney in 1994, who was to be only the second regular commanding officer. Godfrey had a strong cavalry pedigree with generations of his family serving in the 14th, 14th/20th, and the King's Royal Hussars.

Westdown Camp on Salisbury Plain in March 1980—Tpr Rob Bushen, John Fishlock, John Angele, and Terry Winters, the winning troop in the annual military skills competition.

The PSAOs in the late 1980s. *From left to right*: Capt. Bill Walton, late 17th/21st Lancers; Capt. Gordon Mitchell, late 14th/20th Hussars; Capt. Sandy Hoddinot, late RTR; and Capt. Dick Mertens from 'B' Squadron, late RTR. Key individuals in the day-to-day life of a squadron in the 1980s and '90s, both in the TA centre and on annual camp, these officers had often held warrant officer rank in their regular RAC regiment prior to being commissioned.

The victorious and exhausted RWxY polo team after the inter-regimental final at Windsor in 1992, having beaten the Blues and Royals. *From left to right*: Lt Alex Dabell ('B' Squadron), Lt Jamie Gordon ('D' Squadron), Capt. Paul Lucas QOH (adjutant), and Lt Tim Verdon ('B' Squadron).

The officers' Halton Camp in Lancashire, September 1994.

The role had changed subtly from a home defence to a national defence reconnaissance regiment, and these were the last days of the yeomanry of old; note the ties worn with combat dress, the variety of uniform for a formal photograph, and the Kennings white van, which strangely appeared in many of the group images. The officers were expected to change for dinner, the only washing facilities after a few days on exercise being a row of basins in this rather basic training camp in Lancashire.

Cavalry standards were nevertheless maintained with retired soldiers acting as mess staff in a Nissen hut adapted with tablecloths, paintings, and the regimental silver. A popular pastime during a formal dinner was to send the newest officer under the table to retrieve, hopefully unnoticed, the colonel's spurs. This was a dangerous task as it was considered perfectly reasonable to stab the poor young officer with a fork, reverse one's spurs into him, or indeed call for a jug of gravy to pour over the subaltern under the trestle tables.

The weather during the first pan-yeomanry Exercise Deep Gorge, which stretched across the Scottish Borders and into the dense Kielder Forest in Northumberland, was unpleasantly wet. The RWxY with the North Irish Horse formed part of Orange Force whose mission was to harass Blue made up of the other yeomanry regiments, mimicking on a smaller scale the NATO exercises of the previous decade.

'B' Squadron in the depths of the Kielder Forest on Exercise Deep Gorge in September 1994 with two stripped-down and heavily modified Series 3 Land Rovers in an age before health and safety regulations and modern IT.

Soldiering for this generation of the Royal Wiltshire Yeomanry was more straightforward and some would argue more enjoyable. Individual military skills were of a high standard with less time spent in the classroom or on vehicle maintenance and far more time on exercise, which is the *raison d'etre* of the reserve soldier.

In 1995, the Land Rovers were further modified, removing all canvas and windscreens, and with the addition of a roll bar and copious amounts of hessian cloth camouflage, these 'recce cars' could now hide behind minimal cover including hedges and walls. Access to private estates as training areas was the norm during this era, allowing the soldiers familiarity with new and natural terrain, countryside typified by a large exercise on the Cheshire estate of the late duke of Westminster, whose young son had woken early to watch the final battle of the weekend.

Despite exposure to elements that were problematic on long road moves, the yeomen thrived with this new light reconnaissance role, and later in the year, the regiment's new role was formalised as national defence light reconnaissance under command of 43 (Wessex) Brigade. At the time, there was an aspiration to acquire an ARRC (Allied rapid reaction corps) role, but this was never to materialise.

The now derelict training camp at Crickhowell in Wales, which once supplied soldiers to the Prince of Wales Division, was the regiment's base for the brigade concentration, and the new recce cars and Goretex waterproofs performed well in the appalling weather known to all who have trained in the Brecon Beacons. The highlight of the second week of this exercise was night firing of the German Leopard tanks at Castlemartin in Pembrokeshire. The troops in the OPs carrying out over-watch were unaware night firing was scheduled and there were a number of surprised yeomen when tanks were heard and then sighted after dark.

Wiltshire yeomen in the above photograph include Lieutenant Johnathan Ford, Captain David Utting, Lieutenant Charles O'Neil Roe, Captain Tim Verdon, Major James Selby-Bennett, and Major Bill Peck. Captain Ben Adams was on duty supervising the NCO cadre. The adjutant Captain Nick Hunter KRH, a talented polo player seated in the front row, later went on to command the Queen's Own Yeomanry.

The visit to the King's Royal Hussars in Munster in 1996 was notable as the first year for many decades that the RWY squadron had the opportunity to train as armoured crewmen. A formal decision to train the TA in armour had not been made but had been discussed as a possibility; following a week spent in the tank park, a composite squadron deployed to the small Dorbaum training area to practise the quick attack onto a set objective. This was the RWxY's first exposure to 'panzering' as described by the CO.

York Barracks was an old Luftwaffe camp, and for many of the officers, this was their first experience of mess life in Germany, which had changed little since the Cold War and where a bottle of Bollinger was cheaper than three pints of beer in a London pub; of course, no money ever changed hands in a cavalry mess.

The late duke of Westminster as colonel yeomanry flew out in his Lear jet, and copious quantities of champagne were consumed in the mess, which had

Contingents of the Royal Wessex Yeomanry officers' mess with the King's Royal Hussars, York Barracks, Munster, Germany in 1996. Wiltshire Yeomen in the photograph include Lt Johnathan Ford, Capt. David Utting, Lt Charles O'Neil Roe, Capt. Tim Verdon, Maj. James Selby-Bennett, and Maj. Bill Peck. Capt. Ben Adams was on duty supervising the NCO cadre. The adjutant, Capt. Nick Hunter KRH, a talented polo player seated in the front row, later went on to command the Queen's Own Yeomanry.

dispatched the KRH horsebox to France over the middle weekend to purchase 1,000 bottles.

In the early 1990s, 'B' Squadron regularly took a group of soldiers for winter adventure training in Scotland named Exercise Arctic Hare. The weather was frequently shocking with fog and horizontal rain, and in 1996, Exercise Snow Fox was formulated with the aim of promoting alpine skiing and ski racing in European rather than traditional British conditions. Devised and administered as exercise director for many years by Staff Sergeant (later Major) Jonathan Ford, Snow Fox was and indeed remains a potent addition to the key task of recruitment and retention throughout the yeomanry.

Major Jonny Payne, an experienced and talented skier who commanded 'B' Squadron RWxY, won the Yeomanry Challenge Cup for fastest male skier on Exercise Snow Fox in Verbier. Prize-giving took place in the subterranean Tara Club.

The Royal Armoured Corps had been skiing in Verbier in Switzerland for decades before the yeomanry arrived in 1999. At that time, the resort was still the chalet capital of the Alps before the fall in the value of sterling and a rapid influx of wealth led to the pan-yeomanry Exercise Snow Fox being moved to Kitzbühel

Two very long-serving Royal Wiltshire Yeomen during troop tests in the late 1990s—Sgt Martin Trott (currently secretary of the RWY Association) and Lt Patrick Long (Colonel Yeomanry in 2017). Troop tests involved a round robin of military tasks, such as testing basic RAC skills, including vehicle recovery (which would inevitably take place in knee-deep mud or water) and first aid (which was once made more realistic by the delivery of some offal from the local hunt kennels).

Throughout the 1980s and 1990s, Gibraltar continues to prove useful for overseas training, the attraction to many yeomen being the chance to escape from the familiarity and variable weather associated with Salisbury Plain. Exercise Marble Tor allowed a composite squadron or troop to practise infantry skills, fighting in the tunnels beneath the Rock.

Above: Sergeant-Major Andrew Turner instructing on the general-purpose machine gun (GPMG). Andy Turner, originally from Sheffield, joined the regular army at the Army Apprentice College in Harrogate and worked as a radio-telegraphist in the Royal Signals from 1977–1987. He served in Rhodesia in 1979 and 1980 and during the Falklands Conflict in 1982, joining 'B' Squadron in 1992; he was squadron sergeant-major from 2002–2005.

Below: Cpl Paul Cross in the driver's seat and his brother, S/Sgt David Cross, from Netheravon. They joined 'B' Squadron together in April 1992; David served in the Royal Wessex Yeomanry for twenty-three years, and Paul continues to serve in the squadron. Their father, Cpl Michael Cross, served from 1971 until just before his sons enlisted in 1994, and their uncle, David Owen, served in 'A' Squadron in Swindon.

In the early 1990s, 'B' Squadron regularly took a group of soldiers for winter adventure training in Scotland named Exercise Arctic Hare. The weather was frequently shocking with fog and horizontal rain, and in 1996, Exercise Snow Fox was formulated with the aim of promoting alpine skiing and ski racing in European rather than traditional British conditions. Devised and administered as exercise director for many years by S/Sgt (later Maj.) Jonathan Ford, Snow Fox was and indeed remains a potent addition to the key task of recruitment and retention throughout the yeomanry.

Maj. Jonny Payne, an experienced and talented skier who commanded 'B' Squadron RWxY, winning the Yeomanry Challenge Cup for fastest male skier on Exercise Snow Fox in Verbier. Prize-giving took place in the subterranean Tara Club.

and finally Val d'Isère, where it continues to flourish. The criteria for selection for this desirable week of adventure training are now strict; all military training qualifications and commitments must have been achieved before a soldier will be offered a place.

In 1998, the imminent strategic defence review led to great uncertainty and even rumours of disbandment of either the entire regiment or individual squadrons, but training continued. Lt-Col. James Selby-Bennett, a Dorset solicitor, possessed a razor-sharp mind and a flair for devising unusual and interesting training to keep away the main threat to reservists—boredom.

In April, the regiment deployed to Jersey to practise long-range radio communications between Germany and the UK. Looking back at this period (which pre-dated the digital era), it is almost beyond comprehension to recall how metal chain link fences were routinely utilised to extend the available radio antennae and thereby improve signal transmission. This is now as alien to the digital soldier as the use of signalling flags in the 1800s.

As a fluent French speaker, this dynamic CO also achieved an unusual exchange exercise with the French Army's *1er–2e Régiment de Chasseurs*, which involved a long road move to Verdun in northern France, where the thirsty yeomen of Wiltshire were intrigued by the draught Kronenbourg lager available in the French cookhouse. The return road move to Dorset was exhausting but made more interesting when, having left the French camp, it was apparent that one of the squadrons had forgotten to wake the squadron leader who rejoined the convoy later that day.

Unusually, annual training this year was split into two phases—Exercise Flying Cast involved acting as enemy to the Queen's Own Yeomanry and a troop of the 9th/12th Lancers; the real enemy was, however, the weather in the Welsh borders with incessant rain and thick mud.

Lt-Col. James Selby-Bennett (right) wearing traditional alpine attire with the former commanding officer, Col. Oliver Chamberlain. 'SB' is a talented caricaturist and a series of accurate sketches were produced on race days which captured the family atmosphere of Exercise Snow Fox. Yeomanry officers skiing in tweed and a regimental tie was a not uncommon sight in Verbier; 'if it's good enough for the mountains of Scotland, it's good enough for the Alps.'

The much-missed 'Col. Gerald', His Grace the late duke of Westminster, who had served with the Queen's Own Yeomanry from trooper to major-general, although not a skier himself, was a strong supporter of yeomanry skiing and a regular visitor to Exercise Snow Fox. Numerous commanding officers and visitors to the exercise enjoyed the convenience of his private plane over a decade when yeomanry skiing went from strength to strength. The author can recall the duke visiting the officers in the Farm Club, Verbier's smartest nightclub, still wearing his London suit.

RHQ was based in a farmyard outside Tenbury Wells in Shropshire, a pleasant market town that conveniently had a Waitrose supermarket, which kept the commanding officer happy. When visited by a Highland regiment brigadier who was offered a plate of smoked salmon and a glass of champagne, the comment was heard, 'I am not sure if we are both serving in the same Army.'

The year ended with the news that the RWxY had survived the defence review with two new roles, providing Challenger 2 crew for the Regular Army and developing the doctrine for armour replacement.

The early 2000s was a period of confusion; what was the role of a Royal Wessex Yeoman? The acquisition of a Dorset squadron (Dorset Yeomanry) wearing a black beret and black coveralls—whose jealously guarded role as an armoured replacement squadron was completely unrelated to the other three squadrons—did not lead to initial harmony.

Over the next ten years, there was much discussion within the RAC about the Royal Wessex Yeomanry crewing Challenger tanks as individual replacements in time of conflict or indeed to backfill gaps in regular regiments when required.

The building blocks for this dramatic change had been put in place in Munster in 1996 while training with Challenger 1 and as the RWY entered its third century it became apparent that the future was with armour and more specifically Challenger 2.

On 12 May 2001, the RWxY became the first TA regiment to complete a main battle tank firing period since the 1960s despite no official ammunition allowance. The crew training at this point was embryonic, and some of the soldiers (including Corporal Cross, who described the controls as 'a stroll in the park if you know how to handle a Sony PlayStation') travelled to Germany to gain turret qualifications.

The year 2001 saw the arrival of foot and mouth disease, and many 'B' Squadron soldiers with a background in agriculture were involved at the front line with the deeply unpleasant task of slaughtering affected stock.

Badminton horse trials continued to be an important part of the regimental calendar, and the addition of a KRH Challenger tank to the yeomanry tent brought more than an admiring glance from camp followers and grooms; the PSI was heard to comment that 'more jumps took place in the regimental horsebox than on the entire cross-country course'.

The sixtieth anniversary of El Alamein and HM the Queen's Golden Jubilee in 2002 were both marked by squadron involvement, but from 2003 onwards, training and administration for the individual replacements mobilised for operations in Iraq became a priority. Colonel John Peel, a stalwart Royal Wiltshire Yeoman, also stepped down from his role as regimental honorary colonel.

HRH the Earl of Wessex visited his new regiment as royal honorary colonel in 2004, observing Challenger 2 live firing and enjoying his first formal dinner at the 'Bovington Hilton', the 1960s eyesore of an officer's mess of the Royal Armoured Corps. The earl's genuine support for his first allocated regiment has been a source of great pride to the regiment, his uniform being that of the senior squadron —the RWY.

Major Patrick Long left the squadron in 2004 following twenty-two years of service from trooper onwards, but he was destined for greater things together with two other squadron leaders from this era, who were all promoted to lieutenant colonel. 'B' Squadron in the late 1990s and early 2000s was certainly at its military peak.

Routine training and continued deployments to Iraq while attached to regular cavalry regiments continued in 2005 as the 'Future Army Structure' (yet another defence review that changed name each decade) confirmed an increase in the size of the regiment against a picture of cutbacks in other parts of the TA. The armoured training had, however, taken its toll on regimental cohesion by creating an unmanageable and busy programme that inevitably fragmented attendance.

As the 2000s progressed, the conflict in the desert continued, as did day-to-day life in the squadron, but in 2006, Major Jonny Payne (as always, brimming with

Cpl Darren Hill leading a river crossing on troop tests in 2000 in an era before health and safety inspectors. WO2 Hill, Darren, known as 'Benny', joined 'B' Squadron in 1995 and served in two appointments as SSM in Salisbury. His wife also served in 'B' Squadron as a chef, requiring complex childcare arrangements. A keen skier, he completed the annual skiing exercise in 2003 with broken ribs following a fall on the first day, commenting that 'it hurt like hell but having come this far he was not going to lounge around in the chalet'. He started to compete in triathlons in his forties.

enthusiasm) entered a team for the fearsome Bataan Memorial Death March—a 26-mile race across the New Mexico desert carrying 45 pounds of kit.

In 2008, the RWxY travelled to Texas to train with a National Guard armoured regiment. The desert training area at Fort Hood, which housed two full US divisions, was vast and the yeomen were given a squadron of M1 Abrams tanks together with unlimited small arms ammunition.

Major Jonny Payne and 'B' Squadron 2IC Captain (now Lieutenant-Colonel) Charles O'Neil Roe led a composite infantry company providing opposition for the armour. The weather was unusual; on arrival, it was cold and wet and not dissimilar to Salisbury plain, and the turbine engines on the Abrams tanks were a popular source of warmth after the initial downpour. Thereafter, the Texan sun appeared, and the terrain revealed the threat about which the troops had all been briefed—scorpions, rattlesnakes, and fire ants. The Texas National Guard were very proud of their cowboy heritage and were very keen to demonstrate prowess with the lasso and snake-catching; the individual who caught the rattler was, to the amusement of the yeomen, bitten and taken to hospital.

Operational tours continued into 2009, but at the end of the calendar year, Whitehall announced a £20 million cut to the TA budget to focus spending on operational commitments, which was somewhat illogical as a significant number of reservists were regularly deploying overseas.

This was a testing time for the RWY and, cynically, the fourth time the RWY have had the axe poised above the three feathers, but the soldiers remained loyal to their chain of command and continued to attend and train, often travelling significant distances without pay; thankfully, this flawed decision from Whitehall was soon reversed.

Afghanistan now more than ever dominated operational deployments and also acted as a potent drive to recruitment. WO2 Bedford, Sergeant Timmins, and

Corporal Houghton returned from that theatre as part of the yeomanry contingent, providing detachment commanders and operators for a suite of surveillance assets known as Cortez, which were essentially CCTV cameras on a large pole providing long-range reconnaissance. Parallels could be drawn with the short-lived interest in searchlights in 1941, and the camera was soon to be superseded by the drone.

Wiltshire yeomen have deployed as individual reservists throughout the recent conflicts in Iraq and Afghanistan, some volunteering for numerous operational tours. These conflicts resulted in a surge in young men and women enlisting on weekday training nights prior to the recruitment process being outsourced to the privately run Capita Group. The regimental medical officer based at the squadron was certainly extraordinarily busy seeing potential recruits throughout this decade.

Some of the fiercest battles of the Afghanistan conflict were fought in 2009, and both WO2 Welsh and Captain Henry Kemp-Gee were actively fighting during Operation Panther's Claw in Helmand.

In June 2011, the RWxY celebrated its fortieth birthday, and as the withdrawal from Afghanistan loomed, the focus of training switched from providing individual reservists crewing a diverse array of wheeled and tracked platforms, to providing trained and competent tank crew, a highly technical trade and of vital importance to the MOD. This was an output that could be measured, and as with any aspect of the public sector, in 2012, the regiment was set a target to provide eight crews a year trained to a standard suitable for mobilisation. Within two years, this target had been exceeded.

Capt. (later Maj.) John Morgan is pictured wearing 'blues' and a scarlet forage cap with an original silver Victorian cross belt. Having started his TA career in the King's Regiment, he served as a forward air controller badged to the RWY and went on to command 'A' Squadron RWxY before becoming regimental second in command. He finished his long reserve career attached to UKSF (R) and is an authority on military uniform. (*Photographs courtesy of Major John Morgan TD*)

12

Freedom Parades and the RWY Squadrons Reunite Under A New Cap Badge

1994: The Year of the Yeomanry

The highlight of the year that celebrated 200 years since the raising of the yeomanry was the combined parade in front of Her Majesty the Queen and HRH the Duke of Edinburgh in Windsor Great Park, held over the weekend of 16 and 17 April.

Representative troops from fifty-two yeomanry regiments were on parade, which was modelled on the 1977 Silver Jubilee parade held in Germany. The mounted escort during the inspection was Wiltshire heavy, led by Lt-Col. James Arkell, followed by Captain Bill Peck of 'B' Squadron and the late Captain Philip Ashton-Johnston from 'A' Squadron.

Thirteen other ranks, including Sergeant Pulford from 'A' Squadron (a keen horseman), followed; an observer described the parade style as 'somewhere between Trooping the Colour and a point-to-point'.

On Saturday, 2 July 1994, the freedom of Devizes was granted to both squadrons as part of the bicentenary celebrations. Devizes has always had a strong military heritage dating back to Cromwellian times, when in 1643, the Royalists and Parliamentarians fought at Roundway Down.

In 1878, Le Marchant barracks was opened in the town as the depot of the Wiltshire Regiment (Duke of Edinburgh's), but the importance to the RWY is the historic Bear Hotel where the regiment was first raised in 1794 and where the annual association lunch takes place in December each year.

The two squadrons marched on behind the bands of the Royal Yeomanry and Royal Wessex Yeomanry, following which the lord-lieutenant of Wiltshire and the mayoral party arrived. An illuminated scroll from the mayor, councillors, and burghers was presented, and following a traditional drumhead service, the squadrons drove past to the regimental quick march 'God bless the Prince of Wales'.

The guidon of the senior regiment of yeomanry cavalry being trooped before HM the Queen. The Land Rover is driven by Cpl John Foley as the guidon is lowered by S/Sgt Jim Walters.

Sergeant-Major John Hunt RH (who later became regimental sergeant-major of the Royal Wessex Yeomanry), Craftsman Neil Ashley, Capt. William Peck, and Sgt Andrew Pulford in a variety of RWY uniforms prior to the freedom of Devizes parade and regimental exhibition in 1994.

The parade of armour. An M3 Honey tank passes the iconic Bear Hotel where this story began in 1794.

The Freedom of Swindon

On 7 July 2002, the freedom of Swindon was granted to the RWY; 'A' Squadron was commanded by Major Dominic Guinness and 'B' by Major Patrick Long. The mayor of Swindon and the lord-lieutenant of Wiltshire, Lt-Gen. Sir Maurice Johnston KCB CVO OBE, a former cavalryman, inspected the parade in The Park, Swindon. Following a church service, a drive past of armoured vehicles and Land Rovers took place through the local streets, with the event culminating in a reception held in the atmospheric setting of the Great Western Steam Museum.

The Cap Badge Changes and the RWY Squadrons Finally Reunite

The argument for rebranding the Royal Wessex Yeomanry with a single cap badge was that it should be represented simply within the army as a whole, but this did not really take into account the complexity of the separate squadron identities within the yeomanry. The argument continued that a unified regiment was much easier to represent externally to families, employers, and potential recruits. With the reorganisation titled Army 2020, there was a desire that regular COs who command the regiment should adopt the title of that regiment, and subsequently, these senior officers would serve wearing a yeomanry cap badge but with no corporate identity.

Internal cohesion was deemed to be of the utmost importance with the restructuring of the regiment to consist of only 235 reserve personnel (fifty-six per squadron) plus permanent staff, which could not provide enough mass to justify four independent and separate brands, and so this could undermine the cohesion required of a small regiment.

The formation of an RWxY regimental association has also been debated for many years but at the time of writing it is not a reality and the individual squadron associations continue to function as they have done since 1971. Geography is against this concept; a retired yeoman from Gloucestershire simply has no desire to travel to Dorset or any other county other than his or her own.

There was also concern that ex-regular officers and soldiers wanting to join the RWxY because of its role may not have allegiance to any of the antecedent regiment, and theoretically, the recruiting footprint may need to exceed that of the four counties in which the antecedent regiments sit. Valuable areas that have not received sufficient attention include Bristol and Bath, Oxfordshire, Somerset, and Hampshire. Potential recruits and officers from these cities, counties, and their universities will not have a natural county allegiance.

The Capita/Recruiting Group partnership were also reluctant to fund four separate advertising packages for the regiment, thus limiting branding options and forcing the regiment to overuse other badges as the *de facto* cap badge. The CO's summary was as follows:

The guidon passes the saluting dais, behind which can be seen the author wearing the uniform of the Royal Gloucestershire Hussars. Col. Oliver Chamberlain is far left saluting.

The regimental association march-past the saluting dais led by the wartime veteran Maj. (Ret'd) John Bartholomew.

> The failure to amalgamate the Regiment properly in 1971 (on its formation), in 1979 (when granted its Royal name) or in 1997 (with the addition of Dorset Yeomanry) has led to more time spent discussing the cap badge, regimental identity and dress than is healthy. Certainly, that debate has distracted from the focus on core activity. If that energy and time had been spent focused on the creation of military capability in the present and future, the Regiment, as a coherent whole, would be in better shape. In the current environment, there is neither the time nor the resources for continued debate.

The new cap badge was, however, not the end of the rebranding as a long and protracted change in all forms of dress was discussed; the regimental council finally settled for the new corporate colours of blue and buff.

The CO at the time, Lt-Col. Christopher Macgregor, will be remembered as one of the most forward-thinking and inspirational commanding officers of the RWxY, who championed social media and pushed forward armoured conversion at a rapid pace. Some 200 yeomen were on the cap badge parade accompanied by the regimental mascot, a rather stubborn ram named Ramrod Darcy III, and the dismounted band of the Blues and Royals.

The dragon rampant, a fire breathing armoured beast and the traditional symbol of Wessex, carried on a banner at the battle of Hastings, was chosen as the new cap badge and approved by the heralds at the college of arms.

The Prince of Wales feathers had finally disappeared as a cap badge but continue to live on as 'B' and 'Y' Squadron retained their identity through collar dogs on number one and two dress, and the senior squadron's badge is also retained on soldiers' cross belt pouches.

The proud heritage of over 200 years of service from the country's senior yeomanry regiment continues to be remembered at the annual El Alamein all ranks dinner, and the association lunch at the birthplace of the regiment, the Bear Hotel in Devizes. Long may it continue.

Ich dien.

APPENDIX

Tank Markings in the Middle East and Italy

Compiled by Tim Neate

By September 1942, the RWY tank strength was nine Shermans, one Lee, one Grant, and nineteen Crusaders. The ORBAT was finalised in early October: 'A' Squadron would be equipped with Shermans, 'B' Squadron Crusaders, and 'C' Squadron with Grants.

23–24 October: Operation Lightfoot			
RHQ	'A' Squadron	'B' Squadron	'C' Squadron
1 × Grant 2 × Crusader	14 × Sherman (1 × Sherman operational at midday on the 24th)	5 × Crusader II 6 × Crusader III 3 × Crusader CS	15 × Grant (3 × Grants operational at midday on the 24th)
1 November			
RHQ	'A' Squadron	'B' Squadron	'C' Squadron
1 × Grant 5 × Crusader II	3 × Grant 8 × Sherman	3 × Crusader II 12 × Crusader III 3 × Crusader CS	1 × Lee 8 × Grant

2 November: Operation Supercharge			
RHQ	'A' Squadron	'B' Squadron	'C' Squadron
1 × Grant (Disabled by enemy action not recoverable) 3 × Crusader II (1 disabled by enemy action not recoverable)	3 × Grant 8 × Sherman (1 × mechanical breakdown during action. A total of eight disabled by enemy action only three recoverable.)	2 × Crusader II (1 disabled by enemy action) 8 × Crusader III (4 disabled by enemy action) 2 × Crusader CS (All disabled by enemy action) (Seven disabled by enemy action, only three recoverable)	6 × Grant (All disabled by enemy action only two recoverable)

It is unclear exactly when the RWY started naming tanks, but the first recorded evidence appears in newspaper reports after El Alamein in *The Wiltshire Gazette* and *The Daily Mail.* The story of the *Charge of the Men of Wilts* was released by the War Office in January 1944 with details of the action and reports of names painted on the vehicles. The naming of tanks was not uncommon within the Royal Armoured Corps, and this concept was fully embraced by the RWY; the names used on the vehicles all had some significance to the crew being public houses, inns, hotels, and place names from each squadron area.

Reported Royal Wiltshire Yeomanry Tank Names at El Alamein, 1942			
RHQ	'A' Squadron (Shermans)	'B' Squadron (Crusaders)	'C' Squadron (Grants)
Trowbridge The Lamb Hotel	The Bath Arms The Green Dragon	Devizes The Bear Hotel The White Lion The Black Lion The Crown The Castle	Chippenham Calne The Bear Hotel Soho Inn Hit or Miss The Mermaid

The surviving photographs of RWY tanks from this period show no visible signs of any names that may simply have been obscured by dust or it is feasible they were painted too small to be visible in these period images. A Sherman (T74441) from the Salisbury troop recorded in Major Awdry's ('A' Squadron leader) notebook on 23 October 1942 appears in one of these photographs. It displays a roughly applied 'T'

RWY Sherman 37. The purpose of the large '37' is unclear, but it does appear on two different Shermans reportedly from the RWY during the El Alamein period.

number, a dark coloured triangle squadron identifier and no obvious name painted on the side. Other images show a large '37' painted on the turrets of two very dirty Shermans with some possible signs of vehicle names obscured under the dust and dirt.

During the El Alamein period, the regiment's tanks were painted 'Light Stone' or 'Desert Pink', sometimes with a green or slate disrupter, complete with white undercuts on the gun, turret, and hull. The names were probably painted in black on the turret sides on Crusaders and on the hull sides of the Grants and Shermans. The brigade formation sign, a white horse on a green background and the unit serial number (a white '86' on a red background) were applied to the front and rear of each vehicle. The 2nd New Zealand Division's white fern leaf on a black background was also carried front and rear.

Within the regiment, each tank carried a squadron identifier, a diamond for RHQ, a triangle for 'A' Squadron, a square for 'B' Squadron, and a circle for 'C' Squadron. As the second-most senior regiment within the brigade, the squadron markings should have been painted in yellow with a black outline on the turret sides, but this may not always have been possible due to the fluid state of recovery and reissue of tanks within the battlespace during the El Alamein period. It was also common for the troop number to be displayed in the centre of the squadron symbol, which is evident from several RWY photos in Egypt and Syria. Tanks also carried the air recognition roundel painted over the engine decks.

'B' Squadron 4th Troop Crusader identified by the '4' inside the square squadron symbol with some indication of lettering on the turret below the searchlight.

RHQ Crusader T44767, which appears in Aleppo on 19 March as the CO's tank 'Trowbridge'.

The re-equipping of the regiment after El Alamein was a very slow process with only two Grants and one Crusader delivered to Sidi Bishr in Egypt for training by 17 November, but even these were returned to 24th Armoured Brigade a week later. The regimental strength on the 5 March when in Aleppo were six Crusader CS, twelve Crusader two-pounders, eight Shermans, and two Grants.

Lt-Gen. W. G. Holmes, commander of the 9th Army visited the Regiment on 18 March and watched 'Cricklade' a Sherman from 'C' Squadron firing on the range. The following day the general took the salute at a ceremonial drive past the Baron Hotel in Aleppo where the whole of the 10th Armoured Division paraded through the streets. The RWY mustered twenty-six assorted tanks consisting of Crusaders, Grants and Shermans and the photographs of RWY tanks from the parade indicate that all twenty-six tanks probably had names at this time.

Confirmed Royal Wiltshire Yeomanry Tank Names in Syria, March 1943			
RHQ	'A' Squadron	'B' Squadron	'C' Squadron
Trowbridge (Co) Crusader T44767 The Ship (Adjutant) Crusader T43745		Moonraker Crusader Melksham Crusader T44875	Goddard Arms Grant T24083 Malmesbury Sherman T145693 Cricklade Sherman T14___6

This assortment of tanks was still painted in their old desert colour schemes with an air recognition roundel on the engine decks. The names were painted in black with squadron identifier in yellow with a black outline. The fox head formation sign of the 10th Armoured Division was combined with the unit serial number '86' side by side or stacked with the Foxes head above the '86'.

A small white horse on a green square and white fern leaf on a black square was applied to the turret sides of Crusaders and hull sides of Shermans and Grants, with the white horse forward and fern leaf towards the rear. These tanks also showed signs of freshly painted rectangles to either cover up an existing name or as a prepared area for the application of a name.

With a tank strength now of eighteen Crusaders and eleven heavy tanks (Shermans and Grants), rehearsals for battle with a full establishment of tanks was planned for April. This was achieved by borrowing tanks from the other regiments within the 9th Armoured Brigade, which had now transferred from 10th Armoured Division to III Corps command in southern Syria or northern Palestine. By 22 May, all tanks and vehicles had been returned to their respective regiments for Exercise Patience—a three-day divisional exercise.

The 9th Armoured Brigade moved to the Binyamina area of Palestine in late August, where the RWY received news that they would immediately be made up to full war establishment of fifty-two Sherman tanks.

The 'B' Squadron Crusader Melksham T44875 demonstrating the full set of mid-1943 markings in Syria.

Confirmed Royal Wiltshire Yeomanry Sherman Tank Names, late 1943			
Regimental Headquarters			
Commanding Officer	Second in Command	Adjutant	Intelligence Officer
Lt-Col. A. M. Gibb Trowbridge T149281	Maj. H. B. Blount Mc The George T149440	Capt. G. R. Thursfield The Cross Guns T149514	Lt A. B. Clark The Black Horse
'A' Squadron			
Squadron Headquarters			
Officer Commanding	Second in Command	OC HQ Troop	Sqn Sergeant-Major
Maj. H. E. Awdry The Bath Arms	Capt. M. W. H. Bell The Old Bell T146769	Capt. G. G. Boyd The Yew Tree T149464	SSM J. Pike The Rose And Crown

Longleat Troop	Salisbury Troop	Tisbury Troop	Warminster Troop
Lt R. H. E. Brogden Longleat	Lt J. Bilton Salisbury	Lt P. T. Lawson Tisbury	Lt W. M. S. Jeffery Warminster
Sgt Harraway Shearwater	Troop Sergeant Wilton T145415	Sgt H. Noyce Fonthill Bishop	Sgt E. Woodman Heytesbury T145482
Cpl Kendrick Sutton Veny Ii T149460	Troop Corporal Barford St Martin T146741	Troop Corporal Hindon T145294	Troop Corporal Imber
'B' Squadron			
Squadron Headquarters			
Officer Commanding	Second in Command	OC HQ Troop	Sqn Sergeant-Major
Maj. the Earl Cadogan MC Moonraker II T149299	Capt. E. H. Milvain MC The Dolphin	Capt. M. V. O. Jackson The Lamb	SSM Parkes The Bear
Devizes Troop	Melksham Troop	Marlborough Troop	Rood Ashton Troop
Troop Commander Devizes	Lt A. B. W. Pennell MC Melksham T149419	Troop Commander Marlborough	Lt P. Brittlebank Steeple Ashton T145496
Troop Sergeant	Sgt Mold Seend	Troop Sergeant Upavon	Troop Sergeant West Ashton T146725
Troop Corporal	Troop Corporal Bardford On Avon	Cpl J. Lawrence Lavington T146730	Cpl G. Lakey Rood Ashton

'C' Squadron			
Squadron Headquarters			
Officer Commanding	Second in Command	OC HQ Troop	Sqn Sergeant-Major
Maj. the Hon. A. E. G. Herbert Pembroke Arms T149307	Capt. the Marquess of Lansdowne Lansdowne Arms T149470	Capt. S. V. Christie-Miller Bolingbroke Arms T149476	SSM Goddard Arms
Chippenham Troop	Cricklade Troop	Malmesbury Troop	Swindon Troop
Lt D. W. P. Bluett Chippenham T149373	Lt D. F. Gilliat Cricklade T149466	Lt W. G. R. H Leech Malmesbury II T149293	Lt C. M. Ausden Swindon II T146777
Troop Sergeant	Sgt Ferris Purton T149375	Sgt Knight Rodbourne T145978	Troop Sergeant Highworth T145877
Troop Corporal Calne T149418	Troop Corporal Minety	Sgt Carvey Corston T149384	Troop Corporal

By August 1943, the RWY was fully equipped with fifty-two diesel Mark lll Shermans and there was welcome news that the regiment would receive a recce troop of twelve turretless Stuart tanks (one of these Stuarts was named 'Clarendon'). The vehicles arrived painted in their new camouflage scheme—a base colour of 'Light Mud', which veterans described as a grey-sand, with a black disruptive pattern ready for the invasion of Italy.

The tank names were painted in yellow on the hull sides with yellow squadron identifiers on the turrets. The regiment continued to carry the white horse brigade formation sign and the unit serial number '86' and the four RHQ tanks also carried a small white fern leaf on a black square positioned centrally over the tanks name on the hull sides in recognition of the Regiment's service with 2nd New Zealand Division.

At this time, only a hand full of names had the addition of a Roman numeral 'II' denoting a replacement tank of the same name—e.g. 'Trowbridge' (Grant), which was lost at Tel El Aqqaqir, was replaced by a Crusader (T44767) in March and replaced again in September with a Sherman (T149281). Considering the large numbers of tanks lost during the battle of El Alamein, this would suggest that many of the names may have been changed when re-equipping in August.

When fully equipped with Shermans, the naming became more formalised with all RHQ and SHQ tanks named after public houses with the exception of the commanding officers' tank 'Trowbridge'. All other tanks were named after towns and villages from the troop recruitment areas with the troop leader tank usually carrying the troop name.

On 22 October, a ceremonial parade took place south of Pardes Hanna (Hadera). The entire brigade was inspected by both the corps and brigade commanders mounted in the brigadier's tank named 'Kilstar' followed by a drive past with Lt-Gen. Anderson, the corps commander taking the salute. The brigade then remained at the parade site throughout afternoon captured on film by an army photographer who returned the following day to photograph the individual regiments. Three years had passed since the RWY had last seen Wiltshire, and it fell to the regiment's honorary colonel, Ulric Thynne, to re-establish this vital connection with their local communities. These photographs were sent to the public houses and parishes whose names were emblazed on the side of the regiment's tanks.

T149464 the Yew Tree, Capt. Gerald Boyd's HQ troop tank from 'A' Squadron in Binyamina, October 1943.

Maj. the Earl Cadogan MC OC of 'B' Squadron in the turret of T149299 Moonraker II. Note the Roman II after the name signifying a replacement tank with the same name in Binyamina, October 1943.

Lt Alan Pennell MC in the turret of T149419 Melksham 'B' Squadron in Binyamina, October 1943.

T149514 the Cross Guns, the adjutant, Capt. G. R. Thursfield's tank in Binyamina, October 1943. (*Image from Sue McPherson whose father Denis Fulham was attached to the Regiment from the Middlesex Yeomanry*)

Bibliography

Athawes P. D., *Yeomanry Wars* (Aberdeen: Scottish Cultural Press, 1994)

Baker P., *Yeoman Yeoman: The Warwickshire Yeomanry 1920–1946* (Queen's Own Warwickshire and Worcestershire Regimental Association, 1971)

Bastin J., *The Historical Journal of The Royal Wessex Yeomanry* (The Royal Wessex Yeomanry, 1980)

Bierman J., Smith C., *Alamein: War Without Hate* (London: Penguin, 2002)

Carver M., *El Alamein* (London: B.T. Batsford, 1962)

Bolitho H., *The Galloping Third* (London: John Murray, 1963)

Collins M., *One Man's War* (privately published, 1993)

De Chair S., *The Golden Carpet* (London: Faber and Faber, 1943)

Dudgeon A. G., *The War that Never Was* (Shrewsbury: Airlife, 1991)

Fergusson B., *Wavell Portrait of a Soldier* (London: Collins, 1961)

Field R., *Rogue Male* (London: *Coronet, 2011)*

Gander T., *Encyclopaedia of the Modern British Army* (Cambridge: Patrick Stephens Ltd, 1980)

Graham H., *The Annals of the Yeomanry Cavalry of Wiltshire Volumes 1 and 2* (Liverpool: D. Marples and Co, 1886 and Devizes, Geo Simpson, 1908)

Knight D. J., *The Undress and Mess Dress Uniforms of the Yeomanry Cavalry 1837–1914* (Doncaster: D.P. and G., 2014)

Lucas Phillips C. E., *Alamein* (London: William Heinemann, 1962)

Lloyd-Owen D., *Providence their Guide* (Barnsley: Leo Cooper, 2000)

Long W. L., *Memories* (London: Hutchinson and Co. 1923)

Martin T. A., *The Essex Regiment 1929–1950* (Brentwood: The Essex Regiment Association, 1952)

McHarg I., *Litani River* (Germany: SHN/Plan4Publishing, 2018)

Mileham P., *The Yeomanry Regiments* (Edinburgh: Canongate Academics, 1994)

Peedle B., *Encyclopaedia of the Modern Territorial Army* (Wellingborough: Patrick Stephens, 1990)

Pitt B., *The Crucible of War: Year of Alamein 1942* (London: Jonathan Cape, 1982)

Pitt P. W., *Royal Wilts* (London: Burrup, Mathieson and Company Ltd, 1946)

Pitman S., *Second Royal Gloucestershire Hussars Libya- Egypt 1941–1942* (London: The St Catherine Press, 1950)

Platt J. R. I., *The Royal Wiltshire Yeomanry 1907–1967* (London: Garnstone Press, 1972)

Ross H., *Paddy Mayne* (Stroud: Sutton Publishing 2003)
Siminson J., *Saturday Night Soldier* (London: Janus Publishing, 1994)
Slater L., *Ally: A biography of the late Aly Khan* (London: W. H. Allen,1966)
Stewart R. *The Prince of the Marshes: And Other Occupational Hazards of a Year in Iraq* (London, Picador Books, 2007)
Strawson J., *El Alamein: Desert Victory* (London: J. M. Dent and Sons, 1981)
Strawson J., *The Battle for North Africa* (London: B. T. Batsford, 1969)
The 10th Hussars Gazette
The Journal of The Royal Hussars and The King's Royal Hussars
Under Any Sky (Sussex: privately published Ditchling Press, 1956)
War Diary of the Royal Wiltshire Yeomanry 1939–1945.
Warner P., *Alamein* (London: William Kimber, 1979)
Welllsted I., *SAS with the Maquis.* (London: Greenhill Books, 1994)
Wessel W., *Mit Rommel in dur Würste* (Essen: Bildgut-Verlag, 1943)
Wyndham-Quinn W. H., *The Yeomanry Cavalry of Gloucestershire and Monmouth* (Cheltenham: Westley's Library, 1898)